No Girls Allowed

NO GIRLS ALLOWED

Devotions for Boys

WRITTEN BY JAYCE O'NEAL

Illustrated by Arrolynn Weiderhold

Tyndale House Publishers, Inc.
Carol Stream, Illinois

Visit Tyndale's exciting Web site for kids at www.tyndale.com/kids.

TYNDALE and Tyndale's quill logo are registered trademarks of Tyndale House Publishers, Inc.

No Girls Allowed: Devotions for Boys

Designed by Stephen Vosloo

Edited by Jonathan Schindler

Scripture quotations are taken from the *Holy Bible*, New Living Translation, copyright © 1996, 2004, 2007 by Tyndale House Foundation. Used by permission of Tyndale House Publishers, Inc., Carol Stream, Illinois 60188. All rights reserved.

For manufacturing information regarding this product, please call 1-800-323-9400.

Library of Congress Cataloging-in-Publication Data

O'Neal, Jayce.

No girls allowed : devotions for boys / Jayce O'Neal ; illustrated by Arrolynn Weiderhold.
   p. cm.
   ISBN 978-1-4143-3589-6 (sc)
   1. Boys—Prayers and devotions. I. Weiderhold, Arrolynn. II. Title.
   BV4855.O53 2010
   242'.62—dc22   2010010942

Printed in the United States of America

16 15 14 13 12 11 10
7   6   5   4   3   2   1

Contents

Mr. Big Mouth

A troublemaker plants seeds of strife; gossip separates the best of friends.

Proverbs 16:28

N o one likes a bully. The big guy who walks up and whacks smaller kids on the back of the head during lunch probably doesn't have a ton of friends. No one likes bullies because bullies treat others as if they don't matter, and they don't care if they hurt others. But not all bullies are the same. Some whack you on the back of the head during lunch, but others whack you with words when your back is turned.

The old saying that "sticks and stones may break your bones but words will never hurt you" is kind of like saying the Detroit Lions won the Super Bowl last year: It's just not true. Words *do* hurt, and the Lions haven't won anything in a very long time. Words not only hurt, they often leave scars that last far longer than if someone punched you in the eye.

Think about Siryn, a member of the X-Force. When she is in danger, she screams—*loud*. Her scream has supersonic strength that paralyzes anyone in its path. Siryn's words can physically hurt those around her. Siryn is a mutant, but your words can do just as much damage as hers, even without Siryn's super-sonic strength. The Bible refers to your tongue as a spark that can easily set a large forest on fire. That's a *lot* of damage. When you say mean things to or about others, whether because it makes you feel good about yourself or because it means you are not the one being picked on, it still hurts them.

Have you ever been a bully? If so, remember two things: First, Jesus doesn't want you to be mean to other people. Jesus loves you, but he also loves the person you're being mean to. Second, remember how you feel when others say mean things about you. When someone calls you names or tells other people something untrue about you, it hurts really bad. Be nice to everyone just like you want them to be nice to you, because no one likes Mr. Big Mouth.

pray

Dear God, please help me to be careful in what I say and not hurt others with my words.

"When the bully demanded my lunch, he wasn't just pulling my leg!"

Word Search

BULLY   FRIENDS   HURT   KIND   PROVERBS   SCARS
MEAN   NAME   UNTRUE   FEEL   WHACK

```
D B D F U M E X J F W H A C K L M
S U E G E S G P C D B F Y C U T Y
G E N V P E W I U B C H L K I V M
L O P T U R G H J U D V B N H E U
Y T R F G I O L K L J H S C A R S
Y U Y E W S K V D L X F V N C D R
T G V H Y J I G E Y R T D L K O P
Y J F R I E N D S R T Y U O I E O
H J U P L B D G H F B V D R U U J
T O P I U L G K J T U S B N M R D
F G H U R T F H R Y G U I F J T N
V M F K D I R E H G N A M E O N P
W S Q A D F K N J H G Y T U R U E
K F J G U T F D G J F H G G T T E
```

Secret Code

```
A B C D E F G H I J K L M N O P Q R S T U V W X Y Z
@ * % ! : = & $ ; + ' # ^ ( ? , / } > < " { ) [ ] -
```

___ ___ ___ ___ ___   ___ ___ ___ ___ ___ ___   ___ ___ ___ ___ ___
(? ? (:   # ; ' : > @   * " # #]

Things to Do

- [ ] This week if you think about saying something bad about someone, think of a positive thing to say instead.
- [ ] Think about the negative things you have said to someone else, and go to that person and apologize.
- [ ] If someone says something mean about someone else, try to change the subject. If that doesn't work, walk away.
- [ ] Write down ideas of ways you can keep your mouth in check.

do it

Things to Remember

wisdom

And the tongue is a flame of fire. It is a whole world of wickedness, corrupting your entire body. It can set your whole life on fire, for it is set on fire by hell itself.
— *James 3:6*

A gossip goes around telling secrets, so don't hang around with chatterers.
— *Proverbs 20:19*

Do to others whatever you would like them to do to you. This is the essence of all that is taught in the law and the prophets. — *Matthew 7:12*

My lips will speak no evil, and my tongue will speak no lies. — *Job 27:4*

The tongue can bring death or life; those who love to talk will reap the consequences. — *Proverbs 18:21*

Who gossips with you will gossip of you.
— *Irish saying*

He gossips habitually; he lacks the common wisdom to keep still that deadly enemy of man, his own tongue.
— *Mark Twain*

Gossip needn't be false to be evil— there's a lot of truth that shouldn't be passed around.
— *Frank A. Clark*

Swimming with Dumbbells

read it

Even if that person wrongs you seven times a day and each time turns again and asks forgiveness, you must forgive.
Luke 17:4

Jack and DJ were having loads of fun on Saturday afternoon playing video games. Jack had invited DJ over to play the new Rock Band game that had just come out. Everything was great until Jack lost his temper and threw the controller at the TV. The plasma screen fell to the floor with a crash. And if that was not bad enough, Jack blamed DJ for the mess when his mom came running in. Jack's parents barred DJ from ever coming over again, and DJ's own parents grounded him for a month. DJ was blamed for something he didn't do, set up by someone he thought was his friend. And the worst part was that no one—not even his parents—believed him.

DJ was angry with Jack for lying about him, and his anger deepened when Jack invited other friends over to his house while not inviting him. His anger grew so much that one day on a class field trip, DJ lost his temper. DJ confronted Jack at the museum gift shop. DJ told Jack that he was a jerk for lying about him, but Jack pretended not to know what he was talking about. DJ got so angry he threw a dinosaur at a glass display of dolphins and broke it. DJ got in trouble, and this time he *was* responsible.

When you hold a grudge, the person you hurt most is yourself. Unforgiveness is like trying to swim while holding dumbbells in your hands. Holding resentment and anger slows you down, and sometimes even sinks you. And the more you let it bug you, the more weight you have to carry. DJ did not do anything wrong when Jack broke the TV, but because DJ let his anger grow and grow, he ended up making an even bigger mistake. Though it hurts when others are mean to us, remember that Jesus was beat up and made fun of—and was even betrayed by one of his friends—but he chose to forgive. Jesus wants you to forgive others like he forgave those who hurt him.

pray

Dear God, please help me not to build up anger but to forgive others when they hurt me.

Holding a grudge hurts you the most.

Crossword

ACROSS

1 To hold someone responsible for something

3 A feeling of resentment that lasts a long time

6 Telling an untruth

7 A punishment that keeps you home

8 A tendency to get angry

DOWN

2 Extreme feeling of annoyance

4 Holding _____ and anger slows you down

5 To pardon or grant relief

"Yes, I'm mad at you! Don't you remember that time a million years ago, when—?"

Things to Do

- [ ] Read Luke 23 and find out how Jesus forgave those who beat and made fun of him.
- [ ] If someone has hurt you and you are still at odds, go to him or her and offer forgiveness.
- [ ] Write a list of the top ten good things about the person who hurt you.
- [ ] Draw a picture of what you think forgiveness looks like.

do it

Things to Remember

And forgive us our sins, as we have forgiven those who sin against us.
— *Matthew 6:12*

If you forgive those who sin against you, your heavenly Father will forgive you. But if you refuse to forgive others, your Father will not forgive your sins. — *Matthew 6:14-15*

Make allowance for each other's faults, and forgive anyone who offends you. Remember, the Lord forgave you, so you must forgive others.
— *Colossians 3:13*

Be kind to each other, tenderhearted, forgiving one another, just as God through Christ has forgiven you.
— *Ephesians 4:32*

Jesus said, "Father, forgive them, for they don't know what they are doing." And the soldiers gambled for his clothes by throwing dice. — *Luke 23:34*

wisdom

When you hold resentment toward another, you are bound to that person or condition by an emotional link that is stronger than steel. Forgiveness is the only way to dissolve that link and get free.
— *Catherine Ponder*

There is no love without forgiveness, and there is no forgiveness without love.
— *Bryant H. McGill*

Forgiveness is the oil of relationships.
— *Josh McDowell*

David and the Cheese

read it

One day Jesse said to David, "Take this basket of roasted grain and these ten loaves of bread, and carry them quickly to your brothers. And give these ten cuts of cheese to their captain. See how your brothers are getting along, and bring back a report on how they are doing."

1 Samuel 17:17-18

Everybody knows about David and Goliath, but before David took on that humongous mean guy, he had a much bigger test. People talk the most about when David was king or when he fought giants or even when he really messed things up because of a girl, but few people talk about the cheese. Cheese tastes really good. It's made of milk, and you probably know that milk does a body good. But in David's case, cheese was even more important.

You see, when David was younger he had a lot of chores to do. David looked after the sheep, and he probably even had to clean up after them. One day his dad asked him to do something in addition to his chores: take bread and cheese to his brothers who were in Saul's army. What did David do? He could've gotten an attitude because he had just finished doing the dishes and was looking forward to a break, but David didn't do that. David didn't moan or groan; he just did what he was asked to do. When David got to where his brothers were, his brothers didn't even seem thankful that he had brought them food. So there David was with his ungrateful brothers and a whole load of bread and cheese. It was at this moment that something big happened. David heard Goliath running his mouth about David's people and David's God. Well, you pretty much know the rest of the story. David showed Goliath who the *true* boss is—God.

The point is that if David hadn't obeyed his father, he would never have been in a position to fight Goliath. So before you complain that it really isn't your turn to take out the trash, just remember that obedience often leads to bigger things. You may be asked to do some pretty boring stuff in your life, but God honors your obedience. And who knows? It may be that boring task that opens a door to something great in your life.

pray

Dear God, please help me to obey my parents willingly and to do what they tell me without putting up a fight.

Obeying your parents is heroic.

Secret Code

Cross out every A, F, J, K, L, M, P, T, and W to solve the secret code.

A F J K P T M L K J G A L M P T K J W F A J K L O K M P T J K L A F M P
T W D K L M P T A F J H K L M P T A F J O W J K L M W A F J K L P T N
J M P T W A F K L P T O A F J L M P T K A F J R W T P L K J F A S P T W
L K J F A M Y L M P T K L M P T A O A F J K L W P T M L U A F J K L M P
T R O L M P T K J B F A J K L M E A F W T P T M L M L D A F K L M P T
W J T I K L M P T J K L E A F L M P T K J N A J K P T W F L M P T C J K L
P T A F K L W P T M W F J L M F W T P T M L P T M L K M P T K A E K

___ ___ ___   ___ ___ ___ ___ ___ ___ ___   ___ ___ ___ ___

___ ___ ___ ___ ___ ___ ___ ___ ___

Unscramble These Words

ebyo • loghiat • eeeshc • sosb • iavdd • epehs • yrma

"Yes, Mom, I will eat my vegetables!"

Things to Do

- ☐ The next time one of your parents or teachers asks you to do something, do it the first time they ask, without complaining.
- ☐ When you are asked to do something, don't just do enough to get by, but give the extra effort and do a bit more.
- ☐ Look around your house this week for jobs you can do that need to be done. Do them before you are asked.
- ☐ Have a good attitude when you do your chores. Try smiling while you work.

do it

Things to Remember

If you fully obey the LORD your God and carefully keep all his commands that I am giving you today, the LORD your God will set you high above all the nations of the world. — *Deuteronomy 28:1*

King Jotham became powerful because he was careful to live in obedience to the LORD his God. – *2 Chronicles 27:6*

Even though Jesus was God's Son, he learned obedience from the things he suffered. – *Hebrews 5:8*

Fear of the LORD is the foundation of true wisdom. All who obey his commandments will grow in wisdom. Praise him forever! – *Psalm 111:10*

Young people who obey the law are wise; those with wild friends bring shame to their parents. – *Proverbs 28:7*

wisdom

Wicked men obey from fear; good men, from love. – *Aristotle*

One act of obedience is better than one hundred sermons. – *Dietrich Bonhoeffer*

He that cannot obey, cannot command. – *Benjamin Franklin*

The Difference between *Oops, Ouch,* and *Wow*

read it

Don't be misled—you cannot mock the justice of God. You will always harvest what you plant.

Galatians 6:7

If you've ever watched the old cartoons that show Wile E. Coyote trying to catch the Road Runner, then you know the coyote never gets the laser-fast bird. The coyote comes up with all sorts of tricks to catch the Road Runner, but he always fails. In fact, the traps he uses for the bird normally backfire on him. It doesn't matter if he tries rockets, slingshots, or boomerangs—the coyote always has to deal with the consequences of his actions.

Consequences are the final results of something you did or didn't do. So if you did well on your report card, you might get extra allowance, but if you didn't do well, you might end up getting grounded.

There are three important things to keep in mind about consequences: First, when you do things you know are wrong, you can expect bad consequences eventually. Since the coyote is trying to hurt the bird, his consequences almost always result in pain. Second, consequences get worse the longer you do bad things. In each show, the coyote's injuries tend to get worse as the episode goes on. At first, he may simply run into a wall, but by the end, he almost always falls off a cliff or gets smashed by a giant rock. Third, real life is not a cartoon. Sometimes people get away with bad things and sometimes those who do the right thing get punished, but we are called to do the right thing no matter what.

Sometimes doing the right thing is the hardest thing to do. Jesus knew the right thing was to give his life for the world so that sin could be forgiven, but he still felt pain when he was on the cross. Consequences are a part of life, but the more you do the right thing, the less you have to deal with hurting yourself. If the coyote would leave the bird alone, he still might have to deal with some tough stuff, but he likely wouldn't have to worry about crashing into the moon . . . again.

pray

Dear God, please help me to do what is right, even when it's hard.

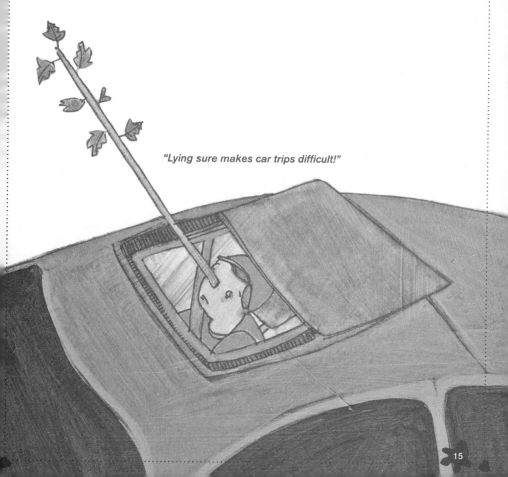

"Lying sure makes car trips difficult!"

Unscramble These Words

Don't be **ldesim** _____ you cannot **kmoc** _____
the **tusjcei** _____ of God. You will **ylaasw** _____
harvest what you **ntalp** _____.

—Galatians 6:7

Secret code

9	11		6	8	8	9		12	5	5	12		12
+8	+11		+11	+17	+8	+7		+22	+17	+19	+25		+12

___ ___   ___ ___ ___ ___   ___ ___ ___ ___   ___

8	7	17	13	7	7	14		7	7
+10	+17	+17	+22	+15	+21	+17		+7	+8

___ ___ ___ ___ ___ ___ ___   ___ ___

18	11	8	14	12	10	9	11		13	3		14	9
+18	+5	+14	+14	+16	+15	+18	+22		+12	+12		+3	+13

___ ___ ___ ___ ___ ___ ___ ___   ___ ___   ___ ___

12	8		21	9	16		18	14	25	10		17	35
+7	+6		+6	+5	+15		+15	+11	+10	+12		+12	+2

___ ___   ___ ___ ___   ___ ___ ___ ___   ___ ___

A=24	G=33	M=23	S=28	Y=39
B=36	H=18	N=27	T=31	Z=21
C=11	I=25	O=14	U=29	
D=19	J=30	P=37	V=35	
E=22	K=26	Q=13	W=17	
F=15	L=16	R=34	X=38	

Stealing is a big pain.

Things to Do

- ☐ Read Joshua 7 and see how Achan's consequences cost him.
- ☐ Whenever you get in trouble, write down what you did to get in trouble. Then write down what you could have done instead.
- ☐ Ask someone you respect for five tips on what to do in order to see more good consequences than bad.
- ☐ If your friend tries to get you to do something you know you shouldn't, try to talk with him about the consequences that will result.

do it

wisdom

Things to Remember

[God] repays people according to their deeds. He treats people as they deserve. — *Job 34:11*

Those who are peacemakers will plant seeds of peace and reap a harvest of righteousness. — *James 3:18*

Let's not get tired of doing what is good. At just the right time we will reap a harvest of blessing if we don't give up. — *Galatians 6:9*

The child will not be punished for the parent's sins, and the parent will not be punished for the child's sins. Righteous people will be rewarded for their own righteous behavior, and wicked people will be punished for their own wickedness. — *Ezekiel 18:20*

A prudent person foresees danger and takes precautions. The simpleton goes blindly on and suffers the consequences. — *Proverbs 22:3*

A man does what he must—in spite of personal consequences, in spite of obstacles and dangers and pressures—and that is the basis of all human morality. — *Winston Churchill*

It is easier to get into something than to get out of it. — *Donald Rumsfeld*

Everybody, sooner or later, sits down to a banquet of consequences. — *Robert Louis Stevenson*

"Help Me, Obi-Wan Kenobi!"

read it

Joyful is the person who finds wisdom, the one who gains understanding. For wisdom is more profitable than silver, and her wages are better than gold.

Proverbs 3:13-14

Without Obi-Wan Kenobi, Luke Skywalker could never have saved the galaxy. He would have been taken out by Darth Vader with little trouble. Without Gandalf, Frodo would have killed the very creature who ended up saving the day. Frodo and his friends would have wasted their efforts in trying to destroy the ring and save Middle-earth had Frodo ignored the old, gray-bearded guy.

Every hero needs more than just brains and muscles. Perhaps more than anything else, heroes need wisdom. Wisdom is more than just knowing what to do, but also how, when, and why. Luke knew *what* to do to blow up the Death Star, but Obi-Wan gave him the wisdom *how* to do it and *when* to fire the proton torpedo. Obi-Wan taught him to use "the Force." Luke didn't have all the answers, but Obi-Wan helped point him to something bigger than himself. And in following Obi-Wan's advice, Luke was able to destroy the Death Star in the nick of time. The same is true in real life. True wisdom does not come from you but from someone bigger than you—God. God himself is the source of all true wisdom.

There are two main ways to gain wisdom. The most important is from the Bible. The Bible is the direct revelation of God's perfect wisdom, and it can help you think about how to handle almost any situation you encounter. The second way is from someone you trust and respect, like your parents or pastors. People who have lived a long time are another great source of wisdom, because they have usually learned valuable lessons along the way from both God and life.

pray

Dear God, please give me wisdom for how to handle the situations I find myself in.

The key to becoming wiser is not thinking you know everything already. You have to be open to learn from God and other people in order to get wiser. As Proverbs 9:9 says, "Instruct the wise, and they will be even wiser. Teach the righteous, and they will learn even more." Even heroes can learn a thing or two.

"Sometimes he makes a lot of sense."

Crossword

ACROSS

1 Part of wisdom is knowing how, _____, and why
4 A book in the Bible that is full of wisdom
5 The parts of your body that make it move
8 Someone who leads a church
9 The direct revelation of God's wisdom

DOWN

1 _____ is more than knowing what to do, but also how, when, and why
2 The source of all true wisdom
3 A feeling of admiration toward another
6 Gray matter used to think
7 Becoming _____ is an important part of growing up

"We should have given this a little more thought..."

Things to Do

- [ ] For the next month read one chapter of Proverbs a day. Keep a log of any proverbs that you want to especially remember.
- [ ] Ask an older person at church what big lessons he or she has learned in life.
- [ ] Ask your parents if you can watch Star Wars with them, and talk to them about the biggest lessons Han Solo learned.
- [ ] Read about Solomon's wisdom in 1 Kings 3.

do it

Things to Remember

wisdom

The message of the cross is foolish to those who are headed for destruction! But we who are being saved know it is the very power of God. — *1 Corinthians 1:18*

Oh, how great are God's riches and wisdom and knowledge! How impossible it is for us to understand his decisions and his ways! — *Romans 11:33*

My child, listen when your father corrects you. Don't neglect your mother's instruction. — *Proverbs 1:8*

Fear of the LORD is the foundation of true wisdom. All who obey his commandments will grow in wisdom. Praise him forever! — *Psalm 111:10*

True wisdom and power are found in God; counsel and understanding are his. — *Job 12:13*

Wise men speak because they have something to say; fools because they have to say something. — *Plato*

Wisdom ceases to be wisdom when it becomes too proud to weep, too grave to laugh, and too selfish to seek other than itself. — *Khalil Gibran*

I do not think much of a man who is not wiser today than he was yesterday. — *Abraham Lincoln*

Singing Praise

read it

In the same way, you younger men must accept the authority of the elders. And all of you, serve each other in humility, for "God opposes the proud but favors the humble."

1 Peter 5:5

Jeff was the best saxophone player in his class. In fact, he was the best musician in his entire school, with one possible exception. Andre was an awesome drummer. Jeff knew Andre was good but was confident he was the best musician in the entire city. Jeff's parents taught him to be honest, so he was: he told everyone in his school that he was the best saxophone player around. At first Jeff's classmates loved to hear him play. But they quickly lost interest.

Jeff was not sure why, but he started to get ignored. He figured the other kids just forgot he was going to play after school. Then he started to think the other kids were just jealous of him. After all, why else would anyone miss a chance to hear him? He saw two girls walk by and he waved, but they pretended not to see him. The girls walked into the cafeteria, and Jeff followed them.

Jeff hurried inside and was shocked by what he saw. Half the school was there listening to Andre on the drums! When Andre was done, everyone cheered and clapped, but Andre didn't brag or point out how good he was. Andre started showing some of the other kids how to play. Then one of the girls Jeff followed into the cafeteria told Andre she wished she was good at something, and Andre pointed out that she was great at math. Andre didn't rub his talent in his classmates' noses, but instead he helped them get better and praised them for things they did well.

Jesus was the perfect example of humility. Even though he healed blind guys and brought the dead back to life, Jesus was not proud. When he walked on water, he didn't break-dance to flaunt himself. Instead he invited his disciples to join him. He loved others, and this attracted people to him. Being humble means not bragging about yourself, but instead praising God and encouraging other people. So use your talents to help others rather than put them down.

pray

Dear God, please help me to be humble, to use my talents without showing off, and to encourage others.

"Third report card in a row with straight A's. And he lets everyone know about it."

Word Search

JEALOUS   PROUD   PRAISE   ENCOURAGE   HONEST
HUMILITY   BRAG   SAXOPHONE   MUSICIAN   DRUMMER

D	B	D	K	U	S	A	X	O	P	H	O	N	E	J	L	M
S	U	P	G	E	S	G	P	C	D	B	F	Y	C	U	T	Y
G	V	N	R	I	E	W	I	B	R	A	G	L	K	P	V	H
M	O	P	T	O	T	G	H	J	O	D	V	B	N	R	N	R
U	T	R	F	G	U	O	L	K	L	J	H	D	I	A	R	E
S	U	T	E	W	S	D	W	D	H	X	F	V	D	I	D	M
I	G	V	S	Y	J	E	A	L	O	U	S	D	L	S	O	M
C	J	G	T	E	H	F	D	R	M	T	M	U	O	E	Y	U
I	J	U	P	L	N	T	G	H	F	X	V	I	R	U	W	R
A	O	P	I	U	L	O	K	J	T	U	S	B	L	M	R	D
N	G	F	Q	B	O	F	H	R	Y	G	U	I	F	I	Y	N
V	M	F	E	N	C	O	U	R	A	G	E	P	I	O	T	P
W	S	Q	A	D	F	K	N	J	H	G	Y	T	U	R	W	Y
K	F	J	G	U	T	F	D	G	J	F	H	G	G	T	T	E

Secret Code

```
A B C D E F G H I J K L M N O P Q R S T U V W X Y Z
@ * % ! : = & $ ; + ' # ^ ( ? , / } > < " { ) [ ] –
```

___ ___ ___   ___ ___ ___ ___ ___ ___ ___   ___ ___ ___   ___ ___ ___ ___ ___ ___
& ? !   ? , , ? > : >   < $:   , } ? " !

___ ___ ___   ___ ___ ___ ___ ___ ___   ___ ___ ___   ___ ___ ___ ___ ___ ___
* " <   = @ { ? } >   < $: $ " ^ * # :

Things to Do

- [ ] *Write down the names of your five closest friends and what they are good at.*
- [ ] *The next time you see a person do something well, tell them how good they are.*
- [ ] *Ask one of your friends to teach you to do something they are good at that you are not.*
- [ ] *Read Isaiah 52–53. Think about what made Jesus humble, and ask God to help you become humble like him.*

do it

wisdom

Things to Remember

In your majesty, ride out to victory, defending truth, humility, and justice. Go forth to perform awe-inspiring deeds! – *Psalm 45:4*

Pride leads to disgrace, but with humility comes wisdom. – *Proverbs 11:2*

Haughtiness goes before destruction; humility precedes honor. – *Proverbs 18:12*

You must have the same attitude that Christ Jesus had. Though he was God, he did not think of equality with God as something to cling to. Instead, he gave up his divine privileges; he took the humble position of a slave and was born as a human being.
– *Philippians 2:5-7*

If you are wise and understand God's ways, prove it by living an honorable life, doing good works with the humility that comes from wisdom. – *James 3:13*

To be humble to superiors is duty, to equals courtesy, to inferiors nobleness.
– *Benjamin Franklin*

Humility is the foundation of all the other virtues; hence, in the soul in which this virtue does not exist there cannot be any other virtue except in mere appearance.
– *Saint Augustine*

Humility is to make a right estimate of one's self.
– *Charles H. Spurgeon*

How Not to Be a Super Wimp

read it

You have been called to live in freedom, my brothers and sisters. But don't use your freedom to satisfy your sinful nature. Instead, use your freedom to serve one another in love.

Galatians 5:13

Love is not for wimps. Oftentimes guys try to act tough and pretend not to care about anything or anyone because showing a loving side can be seen as weak and wimpy. But that's just not the truth. It actually takes a lot of strength to show love. Think about it. All the great heroes do their best work when they are saving the people they love. Superman has Lois Lane, Spider-Man has Mary Jane, and Mr. Incredible has his entire family. In the movie *G.I. Joe: The Rise of Cobra*, Duke risks everything to save the woman he loves. Duke is one of the toughest guys on one of the toughest military teams ever, and even he is not afraid to show love. In fact, he almost loses his life for his love.

The guys who don't want to love are the ones who are afraid. They're afraid that if they open up to people they might get hurt or be made fun of. The toughest man to ever live had major guts because he endured one of the most excruciating deaths imaginable when he could have wimped out. Jesus could have called on the angels to save him, but he loved others so much that he allowed himself to get beat up and nailed to a cross since he knew that was the only way to save us.

True love can be painful at times because when you care about others, you place their needs ahead of your own. Jesus knew this, and his sacrifice is the ultimate example of true love. Love is not just about hugs and kisses, but being willing to sacrifice for those you care about.

There are not too many guys who would be willing to die the way Jesus died. But he was a hero. He was a hero who was not afraid to love other people. To this day the coolest guys around, like Duke, Superman, and the coolest of all—Jesus—all were man enough to love, because love is not for wimps.

Dear God, please help me to show love to those I care about, even if others think it's uncool or wimpy.

"I'm really sorry about your basketball. You can have mine."

Secret Code

Cross out every B, C, D, F, J, M, P, Q, U, and X to solve the secret code.

__ __   __ __ __ __ __   __ __ __ __ __ __ __ __

__ __   __ __ __ __   __ __ __ __

```
F J M P Q C B I C J M P Q U X T C D F M P Q U B C D F J M Q T M J
F D X U B C A Q P X U P M J F D B C K B D D F M P Q U E S U Q P
M J F C B D S X U P Q D F J M Q P U T C B J M P Q U X B R M J P U
Q X E J N F M P Q D F J G C D F J M P Q T U X M P H B C D J M P T
B D C Q U O J M P Q U F D S P Q U X B C H M P Q U X F J O X Q U
M J F D W B C D F J M P Q U L X U Q U P O B C D F J M V P M J F E
```

"Don't worry, Mom. I'll clean it up."

Things to Do

- ☐ Read 1 Corinthians 13 to find out how true love behaves. Write about how you do and do not love in this way.
- ☐ Think of different ways you can express your love to those you care about—for example, washing their car or making them a card. Then show them.
- ☐ Don't wait to tell your family members you love them. As soon as you think it, say it.
- ☐ Thank Jesus for the love he showed you on the cross.

do it

Things to Remember

Surely your goodness and unfailing love will pursue me all the days of my life, and I will live in the house of the LORD forever.
— *Psalm 23:6*

wisdom

Unfailing love and faithfulness make atonement for sin. By fearing the LORD, people avoid evil. — *Proverbs 16:6*

Owe nothing to anyone—except for your obligation to love one another. If you love your neighbor, you will fulfill the requirements of God's law.
— *Romans 13:8*

So the Word became human and made his home among us. He was full of unfailing love and faithfulness. And we have seen his glory, the glory of the Father's one and only Son. — *John 1:14*

Love is patient and kind. Love is not jealous or boastful or proud. — *1 Corinthians 13:4*

Why love if losing hurts so much? We love to know that we are not alone.
— *C. S. Lewis*

The best and most beautiful things in the world cannot be seen or even touched. They must be felt with the heart.
— *Helen Keller*

The only true gift is a portion of yourself.
— *Ralph Waldo Emerson*

Faster than a Speeding Hug

He is so rich in kindness and grace that he purchased our freedom with the blood of his Son and forgave our sins.

Ephesians 1:7

Ned was the new boy in school. Jon told him not to worry about anything because he was going to introduce him to everyone. Ned was relieved, because he had been nervous about coming to a new school without knowing anyone. Jon said that by the end of the day everyone would know who Ned was. When they got to class, Jon got everyone's attention by standing on a chair and said, "Everyone, this is the new kid: Ned the *Nerd*!"

Ned was embarrassed because everyone started to laugh at him. He didn't realize Jon was the meanest boy in school. Jon's favorite hobby was making fun of other kids—especially new kids! The damage was done, and by lunchtime even kids in other classes were calling him Ned the Nerd.

Right before gym he went into the bathroom and looked in the mirror. He had never thought about his big glasses and braces before. But now Jon's words rang in his ears and he agreed—he looked like the biggest nerd ever. After school was over, he went into the school courtyard where the students waited to be picked up or to get on the bus. He sat down and saw Jon coming his way, and everyone was watching. But before Jon got to him, he tripped over his own shoestrings and fell flat on his face. Everyone laughed—but not Ned. Ned picked up Jon's books and asked if he was okay. Jon was shocked at his kindness after he had been so mean.

pray

Kindness is being nice to people, especially when they don't deserve it. Because of Ned's kindness, Jon was nice to him, too. Everyone else called him Jon the Tripper, but not Ned. They became good friends. When other people are mean to you, don't respond with meanness back to them. Romans 12 tells us that God will avenge your hurt and pain for you. You aren't responsible for what mean people do, but you are for how you treat them. Kindness has the power to melt mean hearts like Ned did with Jon.

Dear God, please help me to be kind to others even when they aren't kind to me.

"This actually feels better than chasing her cat!"

31

Secret Code

Add these numbers to solve the secret code.

13	21	19	11	14	14	14	11		9	15	16
+13	+4	+8	+8	+13	+8	+14	+17		+9	+9	+12

—— —— —— —— —— —— —— ——   —— —— ——

14	6	5		19	11	11	9	16		15	4
+17	+12	+17		+18	+3	+6	+13	+18		+16	+10

—— —— ——   —— —— —— —— ——   —— ——

10	9	6	18		11	6	16	11
+13	+13	+10	+13		+12	+16	+8	+16

—— —— —— ——   —— —— —— ——

11	4	15	19	13	16
+7	+18	+9	+15	+18	+12

—— —— —— —— —— ——

A=24	G=33	M=23	S=28	Y=39
B=36	H=18	N=27	T=31	Z=21
C=11	I=25	O=14	U=29	
D=19	J=30	P=37	V=35	
E=22	K=26	Q=13	W=17	
F=15	L=16	R=34	X=38	

"I wish he wouldn't be so nice. It makes me think I should be nicer."

Things to Do

- [ ] Make a list of people who have either hurt you or made you mad, and think of something kind you can do for each person on your list.
- [ ] Ask your friends and family if there are things you do that hurt them, and work on those areas.
- [ ] If you hear someone teasing another person, stand up for the one being teased.
- [ ] Don't call people bad nicknames. If you already have given someone a bad nickname, give them a new, better name.

do it

wisdom

Things to Remember

The LORD is righteous in everything he does; he is filled with kindness. — *Psalm 145:17*

Never let loyalty and kindness leave you! Tie them around your neck as a reminder. Write them deep within your heart. — *Proverbs 3:3*

This is what the LORD of Heaven's Armies says: Judge fairly, and show mercy and kindness to one another. — *Zechariah 7:9*

Don't you see how wonderfully kind, tolerant, and patient God is with you? Does this mean nothing to you? Can't you see that his kindness is intended to turn you from your sin? — *Romans 2:4*

But the Holy Spirit produces this kind of fruit in our lives: love, joy, peace, patience, kindness, goodness, faithfulness, gentleness, and self-control.
— *Galatians 5:22-23*

Let no one ever come to you without leaving better and happier. Be the living expression of God's kindness: kindness in your face, kindness in your eyes, kindness in your smile.
— *Mother Teresa*

Kindness is a language which the deaf can hear and the blind can see.
— *Mark Twain*

Tenderness and kindness are not signs of weakness and despair but manifestations of strength and resolution.
— *Khalil Gibran*

Up, Up, and Away!

read it

Evil people get rich for the moment, but the reward of the godly will last.
Proverbs 11:18

Baseball is a fun sport, and many think of it as America's pastime. For over a hundred years people have watched, played, or even just listened to the games with friends and family. Every player wants to be the best at what they do, but like anything in life, some of the players do it the right way and others do not.

Some players only think about the moment. These players sometimes turn to cheating to get ahead of their peers by taking steroids and other illegal drugs. These drugs do help in the moment, because they make the players stronger and help them heal faster. The problem is that these drugs are dangerous. Steroids can cause all sorts of medical issues like heart problems over time. Players who cheat only think about the short term because if they planned more for the future, they would see that their long-term health is more important than their short-term stat increases.

A lot of people live like this outside of baseball too. Some want only to get rich and be famous, but don't think about the future. What they have not realized yet is that none of that lasts forever.

Jesus taught us to store up treasures in heaven and not on earth. The reason is because treasures in heaven last forever. You build up heavenly treasure by obeying God's Word. God knows what you do, and he will reward those who love him and do what he says—if not in this life, in the life to come. Players who take drugs get stronger at first, but it doesn't last. The same is true for other things. Don't worry about gaining riches on earth because those don't last! God doesn't value the same things humans do. He would rather someone honor their parents and help the homeless than live for money and other things that fade over time. As a Christian, just like in baseball, it pays to live for the future benefits rather than just the ones for today.

Dear God, please show me what pleases you and help me to focus on heaven rather than on things that won't last.

"It's better to give than to receive!"

Word Search

TREASURES BASEBALL FUTURE RICHES VALUE MOMENT
TEAM HEAVEN PROBLEM SPORT PLAYERS FOREVER

```
D  B  D  T  U  T  I  E  A  E  P  R  I  C  H  E  S
S  U  T  G  E  S  G  P  S  R  E  Y  A  L  P  T  Y
M  V  N  O  I  A  W  I  U  E  O  S  L  K  R  V  H
O  O  P  T  L  T  M  H  F  O  R  E  V  E  R  Y  N
M  T  R  F  G  B  R  L  K  L  J  H  D  D  P  R  D
E  U  W  U  W  S  J  E  D  U  X  F  W  D  N  D  S
N  G  V  T  Y  N  R  U  A  G  F  L  D  L  F  O  N
T  J  G  U  P  H  T  B  A  S  E  B  A  L  L  E  E
V  J  U  R  L  E  T  R  H  F  U  V  L  R  V  W  Y
R  O  P  E  U  L  U  K  O  T  U  R  B  A  M  R  P
W  G  F  Q  B  O  F  L  R  P  G  U  E  F  D  Y  N
V  M  F  O  U  R  C  B  A  K  S  H  P  S  O  R  P
P  R  O  B  L  E  M  N  J  V  A  Y  T  U  R  W  D
K  F  J  G  U  T  F  D  G  T  F  H  G  G  T  T  E
```

"My real treasure's in heaven."

Things to Do

- [ ] Read through the Gospel of John. Think about what friendship with Jesus requires and how you measure up to this standard.
- [ ] Volunteer at your church to help the home-less or the elderly.
- [ ] Give some of your allowance to your local church.
- [ ] Don't rush through your homework this week, but really try to learn what is being taught.

do it

wisdom

Things to Remember

The godly can look forward to a reward, while the wicked can expect only judgment.
— *Proverbs 11:23*

Tell the godly that all will be well for them. They will enjoy the rich reward they have earned! — *Isaiah 3:10*

I, the LORD, search all hearts and examine secret motives. I give all people their due rewards, according to what their actions deserve. — *Jeremiah 17:10*

The Kingdom of Heaven is like a treasure that a man discovered hidden in a field. In his excitement, he hid it again and sold everything he owned to get enough money to buy the field. — *Matthew 13:44*

Store your treasures in heaven, where moths and rust cannot destroy, and thieves do not break in and steal. Wherever your treasure is, there the desires of your heart will also be. — *Matthew 6:20-21*

The Stepladder

The master was full of praise. "Well done, my good and faithful servant. You have been faithful in handling this small amount, so now I will give you many more responsibilities. Let's celebrate together!"
Matthew 25:21

Ethan and Mike both worked for a famous movie director. They fixed windows, mowed the lawn, and did other small jobs. Ethan was short, but was a hard worker. Mike was tall and handsome, but totally hated his job. The only reason he took it was he thought it might help him get into the movies. But he had worked for the director for over a year now, and the boss never even talked to him. This made Mike angry, so he didn't work very hard and made Ethan do everything.

Ethan didn't mind working hard, but it wasn't easy for him. Washing the windows and trimming the branches off the large trees were extra tough on Ethan, but that didn't stop him. Ethan just got the stepladder out of the garage and did his job the best he could.

One day the boss called the boys over to talk to them. He told them he wouldn't need them to work for the rest of the summer since he and his family would move closer to the set while he made a new movie. Mike was glad to be done, but Ethan was disappointed. As Ethan walked away, the director told him to wait. He offered him a small job on set during the filming of the movie. Ethan was so excited that he ran home to tell his folks without saying good-bye.

Mike was angry and told his boss that he had worked longer for him, so he deserved the film job. The director told Mike that he may have worked longer, but Ethan worked harder.

Faithfulness is doing your best until the job is done, not just when you feel like being finished. If you're shoveling snow, being faithful is not only moving just enough snow to build a fort, but cleaning the driveway so your parents can park. The director rewarded Ethan's faithfulness just like God rewards those who are faithful over what they have. If you are faithful, God will reward you with more. Faithfulness over small things is the stepladder to bigger things.

Dear God, please help me to be faithful with what I have and do my best even when I don't feel like it.

Word Search

FAITHFUL REWARDED LADDER WINDOWS TRIMMING MOVIE
SET DIRECTOR WORK FIXED LAWN HARDER DISAPPOINTED

```
D N W A L T I E A E P T U E J D M
S U T G E S G P H D B F Y C U I T
G V N F I R E W A R D E D K M S R
I O L T A T G H R O D V B O R A I
Y T A R G I O L D L E H V I P P M
P U D E O S T W E U X I V D N P M
V G D W Y T R H R G E E V L F O I
B J E T K H C D F M T D U O O I N
G J R P R E T E H U X V L R M N G
D O P I O L E K R T L S B B M T P
E G F Q W O F J R I G U I F D E N
X M F O T E S B H K D E P I O D P
I S Q A D F K N S W O D N I W W D
F F J G U T F D G J F H G G T T E
```

Secret Code

Cross out every B, C, J, K, M, N, P, Q, V, X, and Z to solve the secret code.

B C G M N J O X Z B D P M N R B C E J K W C J K A B R V N Q X K D P
Q V X Z B C S P V T J K H N O B C J S C J P E B C J K W P Q V H O B
J B M A C P Q V X R B C J E B C J K M N F P B C J A K M N I Z C B M N
P Q V M T B J K M N P B C H B C K M F B C P Q U B C J K M N P P V L

__ __ __   __ __ __ __ __ __ __

__ __ __ __ __ __ __ __

__ __ __   __ __ __ __ __ __ __ __

Things to Do

- ☐ Clean your room this week—and really clean it (which means don't shove it all in the closet).
- ☐ Ask your mom or dad if any work needs to be done around the house. Do whatever they say needs to be done, and do it well.
- ☐ If you make some money this week, don't spend it all on video games and pizza. Save some of it for later.
- ☐ Talk to people who are very hard workers and ask them how you can be a hard worker too.

do it

Things to Remember

wisdom

He will protect his faithful ones, but the wicked will disappear in darkness. No one will succeed by strength alone. *– 1 Samuel 2:9*

If you are faithful in little things, you will be faithful in large ones. But if you are dishonest in little things, you won't be honest with greater responsibilities. And if you are untrustworthy about worldly wealth, who will trust you with the true riches of heaven? *– Luke 16:10-11*

You must remain faithful to what you have been taught from the beginning. If you do, you will remain in fellowship with the Son and with the Father. *– 1 John 2:24*

Work with enthusiasm, as though you were working for the Lord rather than for people. *– Ephesians 6:7*

But the Lord is faithful; he will strengthen you and guard you from the evil one. *– 2 Thessalonians 3:3*

Be faithful in small things because it is in them that your strength lies.
— Mother Teresa

I meant what I said, and I said what I meant. An elephant's faithful, one hundred percent!
— Dr. Seuss, Horton Hears a Who!

The real tests of courage are . . . the inner tests, like remaining faithful when nobody's looking.
— Charles Swindoll

The Truth about a Sponge

read it

Never abandon a friend—either yours or your father's. When disaster strikes, you won't have to ask your brother for assistance. It's better to go to a neighbor than to a brother who lives far away.
Proverbs 27:10

SpongeBob SquarePants can't drive, he works as a fry cook, and he has a very funny, ear-piercing laugh, but he does one thing really well. It seems that when anyone really needs someone, everyone in Bikini Bottom looks to SpongeBob as a friend. Even SpongeBob's grouchy neighbor Squidward has looked to SquarePants for friendship when he was feeling bad.

SpongeBob may not be the smartest four-sided creature under the sea, but he knows one thing better than anyone—friendship. To *have* friends you have to *be* a friend. When Patrick feels sad, SpongeBob tries to cheer him up. When Sandy is lonely, the yellow guy spends time with her. Even when Squidward teases and makes fun of him, SpongeBob quickly forgives him. These are all expert tips at making and keeping friends. Everyone wants friends, but few really work at being a good friend themselves.

In the Bible, David and Jonathan were best friends. They hung out and goofed off, but what made them really good friends was that they cared about each other more than they cared about themselves. Jonathan didn't care if David got more attention than him, because he wanted the best for his friend David. Jonathan even risked his life to protect David when King Saul tried to kill him. To have friends you must first be a friend. Jesus set a great example. He was not selfish in friendship. He could've tried to get popular by becoming friends with all the popular people. But he befriended anyone who needed a friend. So if you want to have friends, don't be selfish, but be a friend to anyone who needs one. If someone looks lonely, go and talk to them. If you're having friends over, invite someone who never gets asked to hang out. SpongeBob knows the secret of friendship. You don't have to be rich or good-looking; you simply have to care about people and take the time to show them you care.

Dear God, please help me to put others first and be a good friend.

"No problem—that's what friends are for."

Crossword

ACROSS

2 To be a friend you have to _____ about people

5 Friends _____ each other when they make mistakes

7 Jesus was not selfish in _____

8 Everyone _____ friends

DOWN

1 Friends take ___ to show they care

3 Friends don't care if someone else gets more _____

4 Friends _____ each other up

5 David and Jonathan were _____

6 Friends want the _____ for each other

"Don't worry about it. What's a small bruise between friends?"

Things to Do

- [ ] Read the story of David and Jonathan in 1 Samuel 19–20. What made David and Jonathan such good friends? Try to follow their example in your friendships.
- [ ] Be nice even to the mean kid, because many times the mean ones need friends the most.
- [ ] When you are at church or school, introduce yourself to kids you don't know, and introduce them to your friends.
- [ ] Be a good friend by putting your friend first. Let your friend have the last piece of pizza or be first in line.

do it

wisdom

Things to Remember

There are "friends" who destroy each other, but a real friend sticks closer than a brother. — *Proverbs 18:24*

The seeds of good deeds become a tree of life; a wise person wins friends. — *Proverbs 11:30*

A friend is always loyal, and a brother is born to help in time of need. — *Proverbs 17:17*

There is no greater love than to lay down one's life for one's friends. — *John 15:13*

We can rejoice in our wonderful new relationship with God because our Lord Jesus Christ has made us friends of God. — *Romans 5:11*

The only reward of virtue is virtue; the only way to have a friend is to be one.
— *Ralph Waldo Emerson*

Never injure a friend, even in jest. — *Cicero*

Walking with a friend in the dark is better than walking alone in the light.
— *Helen Keller*

Super Average Man

There once was a king who wanted to help the poor and hurting in his kingdom. He sent out letters and spoke publicly that everyone was to help each other, whether they were poor or rich. After a while the king's top aide told him that everything had gotten better and that there were very few people in need anymore. The king wanted to see for himself, so he dressed up in old, ripped clothes and covered himself in dirt so that no one would recognize him.

On the edge of town the king saw a poor man begging for food. The king decided he, too, would beg to see what it was like and also to find out if anyone would help him. After a while a man on a horse came by. The man looked wealthy, so the king asked him for some food or money. The rich man did not give him anything. In fact, he kicked the king and shouted, "Get out of my way! People like you don't deserve to live!" And he rode away without knowing he had just kicked the king. The king was shocked, because he knew this man—he was his top aide. Just as the king began to get upset, he heard someone behind him. It was the poor man he had seen before. The skinny older man held out his hands and gave the king a loaf of bread.

This moved the king because this poor, homeless

man gave him the only food he had, while the rich aide had given him nothing. A few days later the king fired his top aide and replaced him with the man who had helped him without knowing who he was.

In the final judgment, Jesus says what really matters is helping those who are hurting, because when you help them, you are really helping Jesus (see Matthew 25:31-46). When you help others, especially those who need it most, you are really helping God. And when someone is willing to help those in need, even the most average guy can be a hero.

Dear God, please help me to see you in those in need around me and to remember to help them.

"That's OK. You looked like you had a lot to do."

47

Unscramble These Words

eesslmoh • pgnileh • hcri • ropo • dogmink • hintogn • greaaev • dfoo • gebngig • noyem • codekhs

Secret Code

$$\begin{array}{cccc} 9 & 14 & 19 & 11 \\ +8 & +4 & +3 & +16 \end{array} \qquad \begin{array}{ccc} 26 & 6 & 15 \\ +13 & +8 & +14 \end{array} \qquad \begin{array}{cccc} 11 & 9 & 7 & 22 \\ +7 & +13 & +9 & +15 \end{array}$$

____ ____ ____ ____   ____ ____ ____   ____ ____ ____ ____

$$\begin{array}{cccccc} 6 & 16 & 6 & 11 & 11 & 11 \\ +8 & +15 & +12 & +11 & +23 & +17 \end{array} \qquad \begin{array}{ccc} 30 & 6 & 15 \\ +9 & +8 & +14 \end{array} \qquad \begin{array}{ccc} 14 & 12 & 2 \\ +10 & +22 & +20 \end{array}$$

____ ____ ____ ____ ____ ____   ____ ____ ____   ____ ____ ____

$$\begin{array}{ccccccc} 5 & 9 & 4 & 18 & 11 & 11 & 16 \\ +13 & +13 & +12 & +19 & +14 & +16 & +17 \end{array} \qquad \begin{array}{ccc} 11 & 11 & 4 \\ +22 & +3 & +15 \end{array}$$

____ ____ ____ ____ ____ ____ ____   ____ ____ ____

A=24	G=33	M=23	S=28	Y=39
B=36	H=18	N=27	T=31	Z=21
C=11	I=25	O=14	U=29	
D=19	J=30	P=37	V=35	
E=22	K=26	Q=13	W=17	
F=15	L=16	R=34	X=38	

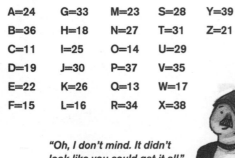

"Oh, I don't mind. It didn't look like you could get it all."

Things to Do

- ☐ Read Genesis 18:1-15, where Abraham unexpectedly served God by serving others.
- ☐ Volunteer for a weekend at a nursing home. Play games, read books, and talk to those who live there.

do it

- ☐ Suggest that you and your family help at the local shelter during one of the holidays.
- ☐ Donate some of your toys or comic books to those who help kids in need.

Things to Remember

Those who oppress the poor insult their Maker, but helping the poor honors him.
— Proverbs 14:31

wisdom

Then these righteous ones will reply, "Lord, when did we ever see you hungry and feed you? Or thirsty and give you something to drink?" . . . And the King will say, "I tell you the truth, when you did it to one of the least of these my brothers and sisters, you were doing it to me!" *— Matthew 25:37, 40*

If you see that your neighbor's donkey or ox has collapsed on the road, do not look the other way. Go and help your neighbor get it back on its feet!
— Deuteronomy 22:4

Do not withhold good from those who deserve it when it's in your power to help them. *— Proverbs 3:27*

Two people are better off than one, for they can help each other succeed. *— Ecclesiastes 4:9*

Three helping one another will do as much as six men singly.
— Spanish Proverb

Unless someone like you cares a whole awful lot, nothing is going to get better. It's not.
— Dr. Seuss

There is no better way to thank God for your sight than by giving a helping hand to someone in the dark.
— Helen Keller

Turtlenator

read it

Lazy people are soon poor; hard workers get rich.

Proverbs 10:4

There is a famous story about a turtle who runs a race against a rabbit. No one thinks the turtle can win because turtles are slow. The rabbit is so confident, he doesn't just run the race, but he stops and talks to friends, takes a nap, and gets some food, only to find out that the turtle has beaten him in the race. The turtle wasn't the fastest, but he kept working hard while the rabbit goofed off. There is a real-life story that is kind of like the turtle and the rabbit.

Jerry had a dream to play football. He was pretty good in high school, but none of the major universities offered him a scholarship, so Jerry went to a small college in Mississippi. Jerry started to turn heads and eventually got drafted into the NFL. Jerry was not the tallest or fastest wide receiver, but by the end of his career, he was regarded by most to be the best wide receiver ever to play football. Jerry Rice may not have been the fastest or biggest receiver in his day, but no one worked harder than he did. His hard work has become just as famous as his three Super Bowl rings and the many records he set.

The Bible states that you reap what you sow. That means you get what you put into something. If you shirk your chores, should you get an allowance? If all you do is play video games, forgetting to take out the trash, should you get to go to the movies? God rewards hard work. He doesn't reward someone just because he is good-looking, famous, or rich. This is a good thing, because everyone can work hard if they choose. Natural talent is important, but it can only take you so far. The turtle lacked natural ability, but he ran and never gave up. You don't have to *be* the best. All you have to do is *give* your best, and God will reward you for your hard work.

pray

Dear God, please help me to remember to give my best and work hard in whatever I do.

"Sure, Dad, I'd love to go out for ice cream!"

Secret Code

Cross out the number of letters indicated and use the next letter to solve the secret code.

__ __ __ __ __ __ __ __   __ __ __ __

__ __ __ __ __   __ __ __ __

3, 2, 5, 3, 4, 6, 5, 2, 3, 4, 1, 5, 3, 5, 8, 7, 2, 6

R E D A K J L L O Y G E W J K U A D E R U Y L G H Y R S S K I
Y R D G L I I H Y R V G R W S E L Y R E D G U O J N F U R W S
U K R O T G J U E S W B P Y G B R E W E I F S C D S W U J T

"What do you mean I didn't earn an allowance this week?!"

Things to Do

☐ *Read Matthew 25:14-30. Write down the things you are responsible for, like school, chores, and sports. Then write down ways you can work harder in these things.*

☐ *Tell your parents that you want to work harder, and ask them to help you to learn how to do that.*

☐ *Make a checklist of all your chores and then check each one off when you finish it. This will help you remember to finish your tasks.*

☐ *Work just as hard or harder when someone is not watching you while you work.*

do it

Things to Remember

wisdom

Wise words bring many benefits, and hard work brings rewards. — *Proverbs 12:14*

Don't you realize that in a race everyone runs, but only one person gets the prize? So run to win! All athletes are disciplined in their training. They do it to win a prize that will fade away, but we do it for an eternal prize. — *1 Corinthians 9:24-25*

Lazy people want much but get little, but those who work hard will prosper. — *Proverbs 13:4*

Wealth from get-rich-quick schemes quickly disappears; wealth from hard work grows over time. — *Proverbs 13:11*

Good planning and hard work lead to prosperity, but hasty shortcuts lead to poverty. — *Proverbs 21:5*

Where you start is not as important as where you finish. — *Zig Ziglar*

Genius is 1 percent inspiration and 99 percent perspiration. — *Thomas A. Edison*

I've got a theory that if you give 100 percent all of the time, somehow things will work out in the end. — *Larry Bird*

Your Superpower

What if you could fly? What would you do if you could become invisible? Wouldn't you love to shape-shift into your parents, teachers, or a Corvette? Superpowers are cool to think about. Guys all over the world argue about who would win, Superman vs. Spider-Man or Iron Man vs. Green Lantern. Lots of people wish they had superpowers at some point. But people *do* have powers— they're called talents. Everyone is good at something. If you are a great singer, that may seem like a superpower to someone who can't sing at all. Perhaps you can draw, or are good with people, or know how to build the Batcave out of LEGOs. All of these things require some level of talent.

Some talents are obvious. If you can run fast, that's easy to see. But some talents are not so easy to find. Tony Hawk was not born the best skateboarder of all time. His brother gave him his first board, and even then it took Tony a while to become great at skating. You may know what you are good at and you may not, but there are two things that are important to remember. First, you are good at *something*. God gives everyone the ability to do something. It may take you a while to figure it out, but keep looking. Second, use your gifts to worship God. You don't have to be a pastor to worship God with your talents. Kurt Warner was a Super Bowl–winning quarterback, and he worshiped God by playing hard and being a good example to his teammates. He also uses his money and fame to tell people about God.

Don't worry about the talents you don't have. You don't see Wolverine complaining that his eyes don't shoot lasers like Cyclops, do you? Focus on the talents you *do* have; develop and use them to the best of your ability. God gave you a talent to be used—never forget that it is God who gave it to you.

pray

Dear God, please help me to discover and use the talent you've given me to worship you.

"Don't worry about it. There is no way I can play the saxophone like you."

Crossword

ACROSS

2 Your talent comes from _____
5 _____ is good at something
9 Use your talent to _____ God
10 God gave you a talent to be _____

DOWN

1 Use your talent to the best of your _____
3 You need to _____ your talent
4 God gave you a _____
6 Some talents are _____, easy for others to see
7 _____ on the talents you have
8 It may take _____ to discover your talent

Things to Do

☐ Ask your parents, teachers, pastors, and friends what they think you're good at.

☐ Write out a list of things you would like to do if you could.

☐ Try new things. You may not know yet what you are good at, so try to paint, sing, or do something else you've never done before.

☐ Read 1 Corinthians 12:18-26 and research how everyone in God's family has a role and function.

do it

wisdom

Things to Remember

One of the servants said to Saul, "One of Jesse's sons from Bethlehem is a talented harp player. Not only that—he is a brave warrior, a man of war, and has good judgment. He is also a fine-looking young man, and the LORD is with him." – *1 Samuel 16:18*

Huram was extremely skillful and talented in any work in bronze, and he came to do all the metal work for King Solomon. – *1 Kings 7:14*

Then Moses told the people of Israel, "The LORD has . . . filled Bezalel with the Spirit of God, giving him great wisdom, ability, and expertise in all kinds of crafts." – *Exodus 35:30-31*

Since you excel in so many ways . . . I want you to excel also in this gracious act of giving. – *2 Corinthians 8:7*

Praise the LORD, the God of Israel, who made the heavens and the earth! He has given King David a wise son. – *2 Chronicles 2:12*

Hide not your talents. They for use were made. What's a sundial in the shade?
— *Benjamin Franklin*

Having talent is like having blue eyes. You don't admire a man for the color of his eyes. I admire a man for what he does with his talent.
— *Michael Caine*

Talent is God-given. Be humble. Fame is man-given. Be grateful. Conceit is self-given. Be careful.
— *John Wooden*

Going to Grandma's House

read it

The LORD is merciful and compassionate, slow to get angry and filled with unfailing love.

Psalm 145:8

Aaron never liked to go to his grandma's house. Aaron didn't like the smell at his grandma's house, and he didn't like the quilts, glass knickknacks, and black-and-white pictures on the wall. He always wanted to play and run, but at Grandma's he was afraid to have fun because her house seemed more like a museum than a home.

His grandma's most prized possession was a crystal bowl that had been in the family for a long time—Aaron figured at least a million years or so, but he wasn't sure. One day when he was at his grandma's, he went outside and threw a tennis ball against the garage. He bounced the ball and it came back to him over and over again. Aaron did this again and again until one time the tennis ball bounced back and hit him in the eye. It hurt really bad, so he took a step back and tripped over a rake he was supposed to have put away earlier and fell down on the concrete driveway. Scraped up and bleeding, Aaron ran into the house. He ran through the living room because it was the fastest way to get to the sink, and the worst thing happened: he tripped again and hit the prized bowl! The bowl crashed and broke into a thousand pieces.

His grandma came in and saw the mess. Just when he braced himself for a punishment, he felt a big hug from his grandma. Aaron asked her why she wasn't mad at him, and she told him that she knew he didn't do it on purpose and that God wants all of us to have compassion on people when they need it the most. She read him Psalm 111:4—"He causes us to remember his wonderful works. How gracious and merciful is our LORD!"—and they talked about what it means to have compassion. Grandma said, "Never underestimate the power of compassion; it can be stronger than a harsh punishment." Aaron agreed, and now Aaron likes going over to Grandma's house.

pray

Dear God, please give me opportunities to show compassion to others when they need it most.

"I hope Mr. Swanson understands compassion!"

Secret Code

Cross out every B, E, F, J, K, L, V, X, Y, and Z to solve the secret code.

B F J K L V G J K L X Y Z B E F O J K L B E F D L V X Y W B F J K L
B E F A Z X Y Z V L K N J K L V B E F T K L V X Y Z J B F B J K L S E
F J U S J K L V X Y Z B E F J K L T J K V X Y Z B E F O K L V X S B
E F J K V X Y H J K V X Y Z O J K B E F J K L V X Y W Y X V L K C J
B E F Z O K L V X Y Z B E F M L V X Y Z P B E F J K L V X Y Z A V X
Y Z L K X Y Z K L B E F S Z B E F J S J K L I B E F Z Y X O L V X N

— — — — — — — — — —

— — — — — —

— — — — — — — — — — — —

"I'll give you a hand. We can have this cleaned up in no time."

Things to Do

- ☐ Draw a picture of what you think compassion looks like.
- ☐ The very next time your brother or sister breaks one of your things, don't yell at them. Instead, tell them not to worry about it and do something nice for them.
- ☐ When you see that your mom is tired, offer to do the dishes for her so she can relax.
- ☐ Write about a time when you were shown compassion and how it made you feel.

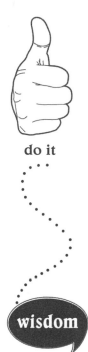

do it

wisdom

Things to Remember

Have compassion on me, LORD, for I am weak. Heal me, LORD, for my bones are in agony. *– Psalm 6:2*

Remember, O LORD, your compassion and unfailing love, which you have shown from long ages past. *– Psalm 25:6*

The LORD is compassionate and merciful, slow to get angry and filled with unfailing love. *– Psalm 103:8*

The LORD is like a father to his children, tender and compassionate to those who fear him. *– Psalm 103:13*

You must be compassionate, just as your Father is compassionate. *– Luke 6:36*

How far you go in life depends on your being tender with the young, compassionate with the aged, sympathetic with the striving and tolerant of the weak and the strong. Because someday in life you will have been all of these. *– George Washington Carver*

I would rather feel compassion than know the meaning of it. *– Thomas Aquinas*

Reality TV

read it

Nothing in all creation is hidden from God. Everything is naked and exposed before his eyes, and he is the one to whom we are accountable.

Hebrews 4:13

On the TV show *Survivor*, a group of people is dropped off in a jungle somewhere and told to "survive." They compete for food, comfort, and money. In order to win, each player has to do his or her best to outplay and outsmart everyone else. The tricky part is that everything the players do or say is caught on camera for the whole world to see. So if Jimmy is lying his face off to win the game, his entire family back home can see him telling lies.

If Steve gets angry, then every bad word he screams is on TV for his teachers to watch halfway across the planet. Not only can they watch it, but they can watch it over and over again when it gets posted on YouTube. Can you imagine how it would be if everything you have ever done were open for everyone to see? If your life was on reality TV, then that time when you kicked your brother for ripping your Adrian Peterson jersey could be watched by anyone who wanted to see you get angry. You could never get away with anything ever again.

But you *are* in a reality TV program of sorts, because everything you do is seen. It may not be seen by everyone, but God sees it all. God knows when you cheated on your history test or when you lied about not calling Jessica a skunk face. He even knows what you think. So when you were thinking of all the things you wished you could say to all of the bossy adults, he knows what was on your mind. If you do the right things, then it won't matter if people see what you do because there will be nothing to hide. Having strong character means doing the right things even when people aren't looking. God wants you to reflect the type of character that he has so that when people see you, they see a solid example of Jesus. So remember, even if you can't see God, he sees you.

pray

Dear God, please help me to reflect your character and do what is right, whether others can see me or not.

Is it really cheating if you don't get caught?

Secret Codes

Cross out the number of letters indicated and use the next letter to solve the secret code.

—— —— ——   —— —— —— —— ——

—— —— —— —— —— —— —— —— ——

—— —— ——   —— ——

3, 2, 5, 3, 4, 6, 5, 2, 3, 4, 1, 5, 3, 5, 8, 7, 2, 6, 4, 5, 1, 3

L O M G R F O F T R W S D L O F S S E H U E Y R E S J I E T R V X I S T
W E J I T V R S I H E G R U R E C G Y P K T T P U J T V H R T H F E I J Y I U
O K M H G X N Y N G P K U G R C Y T G R D O H I Y R D U O D J U R O

Add these numbers to solve the secret code.

8	10	16		11	17	8	15		11	14	5	6	16
+25	+4	+3		+11	+18	+14	+12		+15	+13	+9	+11	+12
——	——	——		——	——	——	——		——	——	——	——	——

9	3	12	20		11	11	20		23	4	14	12	12
+8	+15	+12	+11		+28	+3	+9		+8	+14	+11	+15	+14
——	——	——	——		——	——	——		——	——	——	——	——

A=24	G=33	M=23	S=28	Y=39
B=36	H=18	N=27	T=31	Z=21
C=11	I=25	O=14	U=29	
D=19	J=30	P=37	V=35	
E=22	K=26	Q=13	W=17	
F=15	L=16	R=34	X=38	

"Don't worry! Mr. Brown will never catch us."

Things to Do

- [ ] *Write out a list of any bad habits that you might have: lying, yelling, etc. Ask God to help you to stop these bad habits.*
- [ ] *Read Matthew 15 and talk to your parents about what you learned about purity.*
- [ ] *Write a letter to God, apologizing for the bad things you've done in his sight and asking him to show you how to have strong character.*
- [ ] *With your parents' permission, watch* Superman: The Movie *and see what kind of character Superman shows while defending his friends.*

do it

Things to Remember

Remember how the LORD your God led you through the wilderness for these forty years, humbling you and testing you to prove your character. — *Deuteronomy 8:2*

He knows where I am going. And when he tests me, I will come out as pure as gold. — *Job 23:10*

Endurance develops strength of character, and character strengthens our confident hope of salvation. — *Romans 5:4*

O LORD, you have examined my heart and know everything about me. — *Psalm 139:1*

May you always be filled with the fruit of your salvation—the righteous character produced in your life by Jesus Christ—for this will bring much glory and praise to God. — *Philippians 1:11*

wisdom

Character is power.
— *Booker T. Washington*

Few men have virtue to withstand the highest bidder.
— *George Washington*

Excellence is not a singular act, but a habit. You are what you repeatedly do.
— *Shaquille O'Neal*

A Bike Story

Be thankful in all circumstances, for this is God's will for you who belong to Christ Jesus.

1 Thessalonians 5:18

Justin was so disappointed that his dad got him the blue bike instead of the black-and-silver one he asked for. Justin already had a few bikes, but he had gotten a bit too big for his old ones, so he asked his dad for a new, cool one. He told his dad that he didn't want this blue bike because it looked like something his grandpa would ride. His dad told him he should be grateful for what he had, but Justin just ignored him.

Justin rode off on his ugly blue bike to the store. On his way home, he saw another kid on a bike. This kid was a bit younger than he was, but there was something wrong, because the kid was crying. The little boy's dad was standing next to him, and he also looked sad. Justin pulled over to the side of the road and stood just behind a tree so they wouldn't notice him. He saw the dad take the bike and roll it to the curb and then put up a for sale sign. As it turned out, the boy's family had money problems and had to sell some things to pay their bills.

Justin went home and told his dad what had happened. Justin knew his dad had been right because he should be thankful that he even had a bike when the other kid didn't. Justin felt bad for the kid. His dad suggested that they pray for the boy. When they finished praying, Justin got the idea to give the boy *his* bike. He did, and the little boy was thankful to have a brand-new bike. And Justin was thankful to give it.

Justin didn't get his new black-and-silver bike that day, but he knew he made the right decision to help the younger boy. He eventually did get that black bike, though. He sold his older, smaller bikes and saved up money from mowing lawns. Justin was thankful for his black bike—even though by the time he got it, it wasn't the newest model anymore.

pray

Dear God, thank you for blessing me with what I have. Please help me remember your goodness and be thankful in all things.

"Thanks, Dad. A new ball. That's exactly what I wanted."

Word Search

PRAYING   THANKFUL   COOL   BIKE   NEWEST   MODEL
PROBLEMS   GRANDPA   CURB   GIVE   BRAND   NEW

```
D B D K U G R A N D P A Y E J L M
S U T E K I B P C D T F Y C U T Y
G V N O I E W I U E H S L K R V H
I O P T L T G H J O A V B R A N D
Y T R R G B O L K L N H D I P R D
P U W E A S J W D U K F L D N D S
V N V E R Y R U N G F E E L F O T
B J E T V H I D R M U D D O O Y S
B J U W L I T N H F L V O R U W B
R R P I E L G K G T U S M B M R L
W G U Q B S F J R Y G U I F D Y O
V M F C U R T B H K W E N I O R O
W S Q A D F K N J H G Y T U R W C
K F J G U T S M E L B O R P T T E
```

Secret Code

```
A B C D E F G H I J K L M N O P Q R S T U V W X Y Z
≈ ´ ! @ # $ % ^ & * ( ) " Ï = + Ω ç √ ∫ Δ © ∂ ß å π
```

__ __ __ __ __ __ __ __ __ __
´ # ∫ ^ ≈ Ï ($ Δ)

__ __ __ __ __ __ __ __ __ __
$ = ç ∂ ^ ≈ ∫ å = Δ

__ __ __ __
^ ≈ © #

Things to Do

- ☐ Before you ask God for anything, first thank him for all the things he has already given you and ask him to help you to be more thankful.
- ☐ When someone gives you something, always say thank you, even if you do not like it.
- ☐ Write down all the things you have to be thankful for. Thank those who are responsible for them.
- ☐ Make a card for your pastor, parent, or teacher, thanking them for all of their hard work.

do it

Things to Remember

wisdom

Make thankfulness your sacrifice to God, and keep the vows you made to the Most High. — *Psalm 50:14*

Obscene stories, foolish talk, and coarse jokes—these are not for you. Instead, let there be thankfulness to God. — *Ephesians 5:4*

And let the peace that comes from Christ rule in your hearts. For as members of one body you are called to live in peace. And always be thankful. — *Colossians 3:15*

Let the message about Christ, in all its richness, fill your lives. Teach and counsel each other with all the wisdom he gives. Sing psalms and hymns and spiritual songs to God with thankful hearts. — *Colossians 3:16*

Devote yourselves to prayer with an alert mind and a thankful heart. — *Colossians 4:2*

A thankful heart is not only the greatest virtue, but the parent of all other virtues.
— *Cicero*

We must find time to stop and thank the people who make a difference in our lives.
— *John F. Kennedy*

Things turn out best for people who make the best of the way things turn out.
— *John Wooden*

MegaTrouble

read it

Yet true godliness with contentment is itself great wealth.

1 Timothy 6:6

Megatron is a leader of the Decepticons in the movie *Transformers*. He is known as one of the baddest bad guys around, but the problem is he is never content. Being content is being happy with who you are and what you already have. Megatron is never happy with anything. He is already a leader, but he wants even more people to follow him. He has a lot of power, but he wants even more. His desire for more of everything gets him in trouble. In fact, maybe his name should be MegaTrouble, because Megatron's desire for more power never allows him to be satisfied. His need for glory, power, and control creates a hunger that can never be met.

What if you were thirsty, but no matter how much you drank, you were still thirsty? Can you imagine if you were hungry, but no matter what you ate you were *still* hungry? You could eat 10 pizzas, 24 ice cream sundaes, and 109 cheese sticks, but still be starving. Eating can be fun, but if you were always starving, it would be torture to never be able to get rid of those hunger pains.

Food isn't the only thing people have a hunger for (some may want shoes or video games), and many people live like they are always "starving." God wants you to have good things—until you want them so much they begin to control you. When you are not content, stuff like money, food, and even video games can be like a drug. God wants you to be content with what you have so you are free to follow him. He wants you to be thankful for what you have so that you can enjoy where you are, not worrying about what you'll get next. Megatron is so consumed with his hunger that he becomes more and more evil. He is unwilling to change, but you can if you want to. Be happy with what you have and let God worry about the things you don't.

pray

Dear God, please help me to be content with what I have and trust you for everything else.

Unscramble These Words

ttnenoc • musoncde • aenomgrt • urdg • nvigrtsa • ttyihsr
• tcnolor • regunh • wpreo • rsdeie • ulebort • siefdiast

Secret Code

___ ___ ___   ___ ___ ___   ___ ___ ___ ___
16 22 31   33 14 19   31 24 26 22

___ ___ ___ ___   ___ ___   ___ ___ ___ ___
11 24 34 22   14 15   17 18 24 31

___ ___ ___   ___ ___ ___ ___ '___   ___ ___ ___ ___
39 14 29   19 14 27   31   18 24 35 22

A=24	G=33	M=23	S=28	Y=39
B=36	H=18	N=27	T=31	Z=21
C=11	I=25	O=14	U=29	
D=19	J=30	P=37	V=35	
E=22	K=26	Q=13	W=17	
F=15	L=16	R=34	X=38	

"One more trip and I should be OK for tonight."

Things to Do

- [ ] *Read Philippians 4. Think about the secret to Paul's contentment, and ask God to help you to be content with what you have.*
- [ ] *Keep track this week of how you spend your time outside of school. If there is an activity that dominates your time more than the time you spend with God, try to cut back on it.*
- [ ] *Instead of buying something for yourself, buy a gift for a friend or for someone in need.*
- [ ] *If you get an allowance, instead of spending it on games this week, donate it to your church's missions or giving ministries.*

do it

wisdom

Things to Remember

[Jesus] said, "Beware! Guard against every kind of greed. Life is not measured by how much you own." *— Luke 12:15*

Not that I was ever in need, for I have learned how to be content with whatever I have. . . . I can do everything through Christ, who gives me strength. *— Philippians 4:11, 13*

So if we have enough food and clothing, let us be content. *— 1 Timothy 6:8*

Some people are always greedy for more, but the godly love to give! *— Proverbs 21:26*

You have indeed defeated Edom, and you are very proud of it. But be content with your victory and stay at home! Why stir up trouble that will only bring disaster on you and the people of Judah?
— 2 Kings 14:10

Contentment is natural wealth, luxury is artificial poverty. *— Socrates*

Everyone chases after happiness, not noticing that happiness is right at their heels.
— Bertolt Brecht

The man who is elated by success and is cast down by failure is still a carnal man. At best his fruit will have a worm in it. *— A. W. Tozer*

Being a
Team Player

read it

The smallest family will become a thousand people, and the tiniest group will become a mighty nation. At the right time, I, the LORD, will make it happen.

Isaiah 60:22

Everyone likes a team player. In basketball it doesn't matter how good you are if you don't have any teammates. Even the best players need help. Imagine Dwight Howard playing against five players all by himself. Howard is good, but he is not *that* good. Everyone needs help in basketball, just like everyone needs help in life. God knows this, so he gave you your own team—your family.

There are a few important things to remember about family. The first is that there are different types of families. You have the family you are born into. You also have a church family. And you have people God brings into your life that you adopt as family.

The second thing you need to know is that families are not perfect. Some moms and dads have problems, and some are not around like you might wish they were. And all parents (and kids) are human, which means they screw up from time to time. This can be very hard, but even if your family has difficulties, you always have a family when you are part of God's team. Some basketball players are drafted by a team, and sometimes a team trades for a player it really, really wants. The church is a team full of people

Jesus drafted. Jesus wanted you on his team so much that he traded his life so you could be in his family.

Jesus did this because he thinks family is important. If you have a good family, be grateful for it. If your family life is rough, always remember that you are a part of God's family. Are you a team player? When your parents or brothers and sisters are down, cheer them up, and when they need help, help them out. Some days you'll be the star and other days you'll get the assist. If you are a ball hog, you won't win very much, but if you love your family and want to be a team player, you will enjoy being on a great team.

pray

Dear God, thank you for the family you've placed me in. Please help me to be a team player in my family.

"Being part of this church makes me feel like I have ten dads."

Crossword

ACROSS

1 Some players are _____, a special kind of choosing

4 Jesus believes _____ is important

5 "The _____ group will become a mighty nation"

6 No family is _____

8 Your family is your _____

9 You should be _____ for your family

DOWN

2 You can _____ people God brings into your life as family

3 There are _____ types of families

7 Jesus _____ his life so you could be in his family

"I wonder if being thankful for family includes sisters?"

Things to Do

- Help your brother or sister with their chores when you are done with yours.
- Get involved in your local church as a part of God's family.
- Ask your parents if it is okay to invite someone over who doesn't have anywhere to go for an upcoming holiday.
- Play a pickup game of basketball this week, and work at not thinking of what's best for you, but what's best for your team.

do it
. . .

Things to Remember

wisdom

The wicked die and disappear, but the family of the godly stands firm. — *Proverbs 12:7*

He knew their thoughts, so he said, "Any kingdom divided by civil war is doomed. A family splintered by feuding will fall apart." — *Luke 11:17*

God places the lonely in families; he sets the prisoners free and gives them joy. — *Psalm 68:6*

God decided in advance to adopt us into his own family by bringing us to himself through Jesus Christ. This is what he wanted to do, and it gave him great pleasure. — *Ephesians 1:5*

So now you Gentiles are no longer strangers and foreigners. You are citizens along with all of God's holy people. You are members of God's family. — *Ephesians 2:19*

A happy family is but an earlier heaven. — *George Bernard Shaw*

The only rock I know that stays steady, the only institution I know that works, is the family. — *Lee Iacocca*

Family is the most important thing in the world. — *Princess Diana*

Skunk Face

Young people who obey the law are wise; those with wild friends bring shame to their parents.
Proverbs 28:7

Jessica and Jerrod went camping with some friends and their Aunt Kathy. It was the first time Jessica and Jerrod had ever gone camping without their parents. And since they were brother and sister, they always looked out for each other.

When they got to the campsite, they put up their tent and built a campfire. Then they all started playing Duck, Duck, Goose, which both Jessica and Jerrod thought was childish and boring. After nightfall Aunt Kathy and most of the other kids went to look for more firewood. While they were gone, another group of campers came by and invited Jessica and Jerrod to hang out with them and catch a raccoon they had seen, even though it was against the rules to mess with the animals. Jerrod said no, but Jessica wanted to hang out with them because they were older and cooler than those who came with Aunt Kathy. Jerrod tried to talk Jessica out of going with the new group, but she was tired of the little kids' games, so she left with the older group. Jerrod worried about his sister, and it only got worse when he heard her scream. He saw her running toward him. She quickly hugged Jerrod, and he was glad to see her. But something was different. She stunk—really badly.

The "raccoon" the cool kids were chasing was really a skunk, and it sprayed everyone. If Jessica had not gone with the older kids, she would never have smelled bad. Bad friends are like skunks: if they smell bad, then you will start to smell bad too. God loves to see his people build strong friendships, but he warns against bad friends. When you hang out with the wrong crowd, you can't stop their nasty odor from getting on you. When the young kids came back, they smelled all the older campers and teased them by calling them Skunk Face. If you hang out with the wrong people, you can get a bad reputation . . . and maybe a stinky nickname, too.

pray

Dear God, please help me to make the right friends and to know who I should and shouldn't hang out with.

"No, thanks. Billy and I are going the other way."

Secret Codes

Add these numbers to solve the secret code.

7	10	16	22	17	13	15		11	14	22	7
+11	+14	+11	+11	+8	+14	+18		+6	+11	+9	+11

___ ___ ___ ___ ___ ___ ___   ___ ___ ___ ___

12	3	12		6	11	11	20	23
+19	+15	+10		+11	+23	+3	+7	+10

___ ___ ___   ___ ___ ___ ___ ___

12	10	11	26	7	8		6	11	14		15	16	13
+25	+12	+3	+11	+9	+14		+5	+13	+13		+18	+6	+18

___ ___ ___ ___ ___ ___   ___ ___ ___   ___ ___ ___

27	4	20		17	18		27	20	8	25	18	14	19
+12	+10	+9		+8	+9		+4	+14	+6	+4	+18	+2	+3

___ ___ ___   ___ ___   ___ ___ ___ ___ ___ ___ ___

A=24	G=33	M=23	S=28	Y=39
B=36	H=18	N=27	T=31	Z=21
C=11	I=25	O=14	U=29	
D=19	J=30	P=37	V=35	
E=22	K=26	Q=13	W=17	
F=15	L=16	R=34	X=38	

Cross out every F, I, J, K, L, Q, V, X, and Z to solve the secret code.

FQBVXAFIJDLVXCOKLIMQVXIFXQILPFIJKVAXZNZXI
LKYFIJCJLOQVIRRLVXUIPJKLTFIZSVLGQVIOJLOZ
KFDJICKLHIFVIJFAXZFIRIFLAZIXQCVZTVXEQIJLRKZ

___ ___ ___   ___ ___ ___ ___ ___ ___ ___

___ ___ ___ ___ ___ ___ ___   ___ ___ ___

___ ___ ___ ___ ___ ___ ___ ___

Things to Do

- [ ] Ask your parents and pastors who they think are good kids to hang out with and why.
- [ ] If a friend wants you to do something you know you shouldn't do, suggest something different for you both to do.
- [ ] Read Proverbs 4. Write in your journal (or on a sheet of paper) what it means to "guard your heart" in your friendships.
- [ ] Spend time with your (or a friend's) younger siblings and try to be a good influence on them.

do it

Things to Remember

A friend is always loyal, and a brother is born to help in time of need. — *Proverbs 17:17*

There are "friends" who destroy each other, but a real friend sticks closer than a brother. — *Proverbs 18:24*

Don't team up with those who are unbelievers. How can righteousness be a partner with wickedness? How can light live with darkness? — *2 Corinthians 6:14*

As iron sharpens iron, so a friend sharpens a friend. — *Proverbs 27:17*

Don't be fooled by those who say such things, for "bad company corrupts good character." — *1 Corinthians 15:33*

wisdom

Associate yourself with men of good quality if you esteem your own reputation; for 'tis better to be alone than in bad company.
— *George Washington*

Friendship is the only cement that will ever hold the world together.
— *Woodrow Wilson*

He who throws away a friend is as bad as he who throws away his life. — *Sophocles*

Lip Drips

A troublemaker plants seeds of strife; gossip separates the best of friends.
Proverbs 16:28

Nickelodeon is famous for dropping slime on people. They have slimed superstars and unknown people alike. The slime is gooey and gets all over the place. Gossip is like slime because it oozes out of people's mouths, sprays anyone close to the source, and makes everything very sticky. Gossip is talking in a bad way about someone who is not around. Gossip can be about truthful things, but often it is lies and made-up stories.

Imagine if every time you talked about someone, slime came out of your mouth and got on all your friends. God points out that the power of the tongue is so strong it can bring "death or life" (Proverbs 18:21). Do you want to cause anything to die? If you have ever been gossiped about, you know how hurtful other people's words can be. So don't talk badly about anyone, and don't allow anyone else to say bad things about other people.

Those who gossip can be called Lip Drips because their words are full of slime. Lip Drips often talk bad about people because it is a way to protect themselves from getting hurt. If John says things about someone else to the class, then the other students are too busy to talk about him. Other times, Lip Drips learn to gossip from their parents. Either way, talking trash about someone is wrong. However, listening to gossip and not saying anything to stop it is just as wrong. Proverbs 17:4 points out that those who listen to gossip are also sinning. If people were calling you names behind your back, wouldn't you want someone to stick up for you? Then you should stick up for others, too.

Being slimed may look fun on TV, but it isn't fun at all when the slime comes from the Lip Drips. You don't want others sliming you with gossip, so don't become a Lip Drip yourself by saying mean things about others. And don't let them do it to anyone else, either.

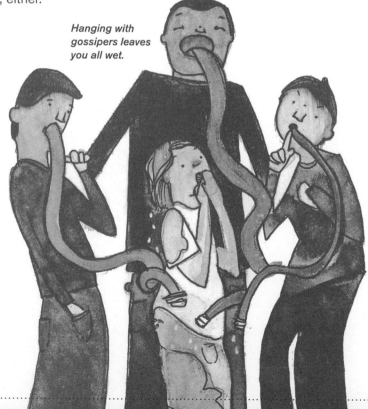

Hanging with gossipers leaves you all wet.

Word Search

GOSSIP SINNING SLIMED TONGUE STRONG HURTFUL
WORDS LIP DRIPS LISTEN PROVERBS BEHIND LIFE DEATH

```
D B D K U T E U G N O T U E J L M
S U T G E S G P C D B F D C F T Y
G V N O H U R T F U L S E K W V H
I O P R O V E R B S D V A N H N D
Y T S F G B O L K L J H T I I R N
P U W S W S I N N I N G H D L D I
V G V W I N R U N M F E D L E O H
B J G T P P N D R E T D U S O Y E
V J U P L G T E H D X V L D F W B
R O P I U L N K T T U S B R E R P
L D W E V O F O R S G U I O U Y N
V M F O U R C B R F I E P W N R P
L I P D R I P S J T S L T U R W D
K F J G U T F D G J S H G E F I L
```

Avoiding gossip helps you avoid drama, so it's easier to relax.

Things to Do

- ☐ If someone starts to gossip around you, try to change the subject. If they keep going, tell them you don't feel comfortable discussing it. If they still keep on, leave.
- ☐ Write about a time someone gossiped about you and how it felt when you found out.
- ☐ Read James 3, and draw a picture of the damage James says the tongue can do.
- ☐ With your parents' permission, look up and make a slime recipe. Cover an action figure in this slime to illustrate what happens when you participate in gossip.

do it

wisdom

Things to Remember

Do not spread slanderous gossip among your people. — *Leviticus 19:16*

A gossip goes around telling secrets, but those who are trustworthy can keep a confidence. — *Proverbs 11:13*

Wrongdoers eagerly listen to gossip; liars pay close attention to slander. — *Proverbs 17:4*

Whatever is in your heart determines what you say. A good person produces good things from the treasury of a good heart, and an evil person produces evil things from the treasury of an evil heart. — *Matthew 12:34-35*

Don't betray another person's secret. Others may accuse you of gossip, and you will never regain your good reputation. — *Proverbs 25:9-10*

Avoid inquisitive persons, for they are sure to be gossips, their ears are open to hear, but they will not keep what is entrusted to them. — *Horace*

The things most people want to know about are usually none of their business. — *George Bernard Shaw*

It is a sign of a perverse and treacherous disposition to wound the good name of another, when he has no opportunity of defending himself. — *John Calvin*

Touchdown Fever

So let's not get tired of doing what is good. At just the right time we will reap a harvest of blessing if we don't give up.

Galatians 6:9

Kurt Warner took his Arizona Cardinals to the Super Bowl when no one expected them to even make it to the play-offs. Like so many times before, Kurt Warner defied the odds. He had always wanted to play football, but after the Green Bay Packers dropped him from the team, he got a job as a stock boy. He worked a few other jobs until he made it onto a semipro football team. He was playing football, but he wanted to be in the NFL, not on a semipro team. He didn't give up.

He eventually got a backup quarterback job for the St. Louis Rams, and in the preseason, the starter got hurt. This opened up the door for Kurt to be a starting quarterback for an NFL team, and he was awesome. Over the next few years, Warner went to two Super Bowls and helped win one of them. He also won two Most Valuable Player awards. But right when things were going well, Kurt got hurt. He didn't give up. He ended up going to the New York Giants, where he was replaced by a younger quarterback. Warner still didn't give up. He then went to the Arizona Cardinals, where he was the starter, then backup, then starter again, all because he didn't give up.

When Kurt's team won the Super Bowl, the first thing he did was thank Jesus. When he lost in the Super Bowl with the Cardinals, the first thing he did was thank Jesus. Whether he won or lost, he always thanked Jesus, but he never gave up. Kurt Warner is a Christian, and by watching his life, you can see that things won't always go the way you want them to go, even as a follower of Christ. There are a lot of things you cannot control. Yet there is one thing you *can* control: you can make sure you never ever give up. You will win sometimes and you will lose sometimes, but keeping your eyes on God helps you to keep trying.

pray

Dear God, please help me to keep going, even when times are tough, and to finish what I start.

"This 'try, try again' business is hard on my knees!"

Unscramble These Words

ltornoc • seol • inw • ahntk • aitsnihrc • ddso • llooabtf •
osaepnser • yrtgni • scradlain • sradwa • ruht • nreguoy

Secret Code

$$\overline{23}\ \overline{24}\ \overline{26}\ \overline{22}\quad \overline{28}\ \overline{29}\ \overline{34}\ \overline{22}\quad \overline{39}\ \overline{14}\ \overline{29}$$

$$\overline{27}\ \overline{22}\ \overline{35}\ \overline{22}\ \overline{34}\quad \overline{33}\ \overline{25}\ \overline{35}\ \overline{22}\quad \overline{29}\ \overline{37}$$

A=24	G=33	M=23	S=28	Y=39
B=36	H=18	N=27	T=31	Z=21
C=11	I=25	O=14	U=29	
D=19	J=30	P=37	V=35	
E=22	K=26	Q=13	W=17	
F=15	L=16	R=34	X=38	

"Yes! All that studying paid off."

Things to Do

- ☐ If you start something, like the dishes or a board game, finish it.
- ☐ Pull out a puzzle of at least 300 pieces and work on it until it is finished.
- ☐ When you have a list of things to do, start with the most important thing and finish it before you move on to the next thing.
- ☐ Ask your parents if you can read more about Kurt Warner at KurtWarner.org or Wikipedia.org.

do it

Things to Remember

But you, Timothy, are a man of God; so run from all these evil things. Pursue righteousness and a godly life, along with faith, love, perseverance, and gentleness. *— 1 Timothy 6:11*

Because you have obeyed my command to persevere, I will protect you from the great time of testing that will come upon the whole world. *— Revelation 3:10*

You must live as citizens of heaven, conducting yourselves in a manner worthy of the Good News about Christ. Then . . . I will know that you are standing together with one spirit and one purpose, fighting together for the faith. *— Philippians 1:27*

Fight the good fight for the true faith. Hold tightly to the eternal life to which God has called you, which you have confessed so well before many witnesses. *— 1 Timothy 6:12*

I have fought the good fight, I have finished the race, and I have remained faithful. *— 2 Timothy 4:7*

wisdom

Little by little one walks far.
— Peruvian Proverb

The difference between the impossible and the possible lies in a man's determination.
— Tommy Lasorda

If I were dropped out of a plane into the ocean and told the nearest land was a thousand miles away, I'd still swim.
— Abraham Maslow

Beam Me Up

read it

"You don't have enough faith," Jesus told them. "I tell you the truth, if you had faith even as small as a mustard seed, you could say to this mountain, 'Move from here to there,' and it would move. Nothing would be impossible."

Matthew 17:20

Star Trek is famous for transporting characters from the starship *Enterprise* down to unfamiliar (and often dangerous) planets. The transporter takes a person's molecules, puts them into a machine, and then all the pieces of the person get put back together again on the planet. The characters trust that all their body parts will reappear in the right places. Some characters have a tough time trusting technology, because they fear that their head might end up on their kneecap and their eyes might be where their nose was supposed to go. How embarrassing would it be if your hair got put on your face? But most of the characters totally trust in this radical piece of equipment, accepting it as perfectly normal.

Being a Christian can be like trusting a transporter at times. The Bible says that God works all things together for good, but it can be tough to trust that God will really work things out in the end. Mankind got kicked out of the Garden of Eden because Adam and Eve wanted to take control of their own lives. People today still try to control their lives because they don't have faith that God is in control. (It's important for you to know that whenever people try to do things on their own, things get messy.) God has a plan for your life, and he watches over you carefully.

However, some people are bent on doing things their way. Why?

Sometimes it's because they don't trust or believe God. Some people, since they can't see God, don't have faith that he's there. The author of Hebrews says, "Faith . . . gives us assurance about things we cannot see" (Hebrews 11:1). You can't see wind, but you know it's there. You can't see love, but you can feel it. Captain Kirk can't see the machine when he gets transported, but he trusts it anyway. God gave you the Bible to answer the big questions in life, so don't worry about the other things. Just have faith that God is in control.

Dear God, please help me to trust you, even when things get hard and I can't see you.

"Waiting until the last minute to trust God might not be the smartest idea."

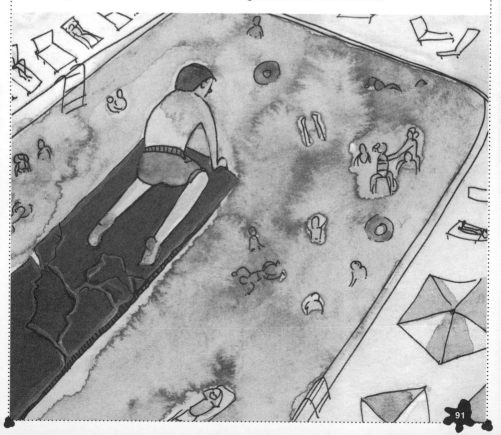

Crossword

ACROSS

2 You can't see _____, but you can feel it

7 _____ got kicked out of the Garden of Eden

8 God works all things _____ for good

9 Sometimes people don't _____ God

10 You can _____ love

DOWN

1 Where you can find "Faith . . . gives us assurance about things we cannot see"

3 God has a _____ for your life

4 Have _____ that God is in control

5 People try to take _____ of their own lives

6 When people try to do things on their own, it gets _____

*"Maybe **some** people need God, but I think I can handle things on my own!"*

Things to Do

- ☐ *Read the first three chapters of Romans. Write down three important aspects of faith.*
- ☐ *Make a list of people you know who have faith in God: parents, pastors, relatives. Then ask those people how they make their faith stronger.*
- ☐ *Read Hebrews 11. List the people mentioned. Look up three of their stories in the Bible.*
- ☐ *Keep your eyes closed and ask a friend to lead you around for a few minutes, then do the same for him, to illustrate what faith is like.*

do it

Things to Remember

wisdom

The LORD . . . is the faithful God who keeps his covenant for a thousand generations and lavishes his unfailing love on those who love him and obey his commands. – *Deuteronomy 7:9*

They fell face down on the ground and worshiped and praised the LORD, saying, "He is good! His faithful love endures forever!" – *2 Chronicles 7:3*

And he said to her, "Daughter, your faith has made you well. Go in peace. Your suffering is over." – *Mark 5:34*

It is impossible to please God without faith. Anyone who wants to come to him must believe that God exists and that he rewards those who sincerely seek him. – *Hebrews 11:6*

Seeing their faith, Jesus said to the man, "Young man, your sins are forgiven." – *Luke 5:20*

Faith is the art of holding on to things your reason has once accepted in spite of your changing moods. – *C. S. Lewis*

Faith is a knowledge within the heart, beyond the reach of proof. – *Khalil Gibran*

Faith is deliberate confidence in the character of God whose ways you may not understand at the time.

– *Oswald Chambers*

Pillow Fighter

read it

People with understanding control their anger; a hot temper shows great foolishness.

Proverbs 14:29

"You won't like me when I'm angry." These are Bruce Banner's famous words right before he turns into the Incredible Hulk. The big green guy has a temper, and even though he tries to warn people, he still causes a lot of damage when he gets upset. The Bible says repeatedly that angry people are fools. Even if you warn people that you are getting angry, you have a responsibility to keep your cool.

The Hulk gets angry all the time, but Bruce Banner was exposed to gamma radiation, so he has a bit of an excuse. Not to mention that he's a comic book character. In real life when you get angry, your reactions are your own responsibility. If your brother punches you in your arm, you can't blame him when you hit him back by saying that he *made* you angry, because you can choose to not act on your anger if you want to.

This doesn't mean it's wrong to be upset about something. If you see Matt cheating in class, it's okay to be upset, because what he's doing is wrong. The important thing is what you do when you're upset. It would be wrong, for example, if you walked over and slapped Matt on the back of the head or gave him a wedgie. God says that the one who controls his anger is wise. He gave you emotions, but he wants you to use them the right way.

When you get angry, be more of a pillow fighter instead of a UFC fighter. UFC fighters punch and kick and get all crazy with anger. UFC fighters also have missing teeth, black eyes, and often don't remember their own names. A pillow fighter is someone who does everything possible to avoid losing his temper. In pillow fighting, while you may be upset, no one gets hurt. The Hulk doesn't fight with pillows, and people don't like it when he gets angry. They won't like it when you get angry either.

pray

Dear God, please help me not to get angry easily and to keep my temper under control.

"I'm really not happy about having to do my homework over."

Word Search

PILLOW   ANGER   FIGHTING   TEMPER   PUNCH   KICK
RADIATION   EXCUSE   CRAZY   DAMAGE   UPSET   BIBLE   FOOLS

```
N  B  D  K  U  T  I  E  A  E  Y  T  U  E  J  L  P
O  U  T  A  N  G  E  R  C  D  B  Z  Y  C  U  T  U
I  V  N  O  I  E  W  I  U  E  O  S  A  K  R  V  N
T  O  P  E  L  B  I  B  J  O  D  V  B  R  R  N  C
A  T  R  F  G  B  O  P  K  L  J  K  D  I  C  R  H
I  U  E  G  A  M  A  D  I  U  X  F  I  D  N  D  S
D  G  V  W  Y  R  R  U  N  L  F  U  D  C  F  O  R
A  J  G  T  E  H  F  D  R  M  L  D  P  O  K  Y  E
R  J  U  P  L  F  O  O  L  S  X  O  L  S  U  W  Y
R  O  M  I  U  L  E  K  J  T  U  S  W  B  E  R  P
W  E  F  Q  B  E  X  C  U  S  E  S  I  F  D  T  N
T  M  F  O  U  R  C  B  H  K  L  E  P  I  O  R  P
W  S  Q  A  D  G  N  I  T  H  G  I  F  U  R  W  D
K  F  J  G  U  T  F  D  G  J  F  H  G  G  T  T  E
```

"Oh no! Who says God doesn't have a sense of humor?"

96

Things to Do

- [ ] *If you start to get angry, count to ten. If you are still angry, go to another room and try to cool down.*
- [ ] *The next time you are mad at your parents, brother, or sister, try telling them you love them. It is hard to stay mad when you say, "I love you."*
- [ ] *Draw a picture of how you look when you get angry. See how silly you can look.*
- [ ] *Avoid gamma radiation, as this leads to big green guy anger issues.*

do it

Things to Remember

Don't sin by letting anger control you. Think about it overnight and remain silent.
— *Psalm 4:4*

His anger lasts only a moment, but his favor lasts a lifetime! Weeping may last through the night, but joy comes with the morning.
— *Psalm 30:5*

Understand this, my dear brothers and sisters: You must all be quick to listen, slow to speak, and slow to get angry. Human anger does not produce the righteousness God desires.
— *James 1:19-20*

Control your temper, for anger labels you a fool.
— *Ecclesiastes 7:9*

And "don't sin by letting anger control you." Don't let the sun go down while you are still angry, for anger gives a foothold to the devil. — *Ephesians 4:26-27*

wisdom

A man is about as big as the things that make him angry.
— *Winston Churchill*

For every minute you are angry you lose sixty seconds of happiness.
— *Ralph Waldo Emerson*

People who fly into a rage always make a bad landing.
— *Will Rogers*

A Still Loud Voice

read it

I will maintain my innocence without wavering. My conscience is clear for as long as I live.

Job 27:6

Robert always wanted to climb the path near the Secret River, but the sign said, "DANGER: KEEP OUT!" One day Robert decided to ignore the warning sign. He walked past the sign and the large boulder and even went past the big tree. Robert got worried, so he stopped. He heard his conscience telling him to turn back, but he was curious as to where the path led. Then, right when he was arguing with himself, he heard a howl. Robert wasn't sure what it was, but he didn't wait around to find out. He ran back home as fast as he could.

The next day Robert went back to the path. He had gotten scared the last time, but he was determined to find out where the path went, even though the sign warned him not to and he knew he shouldn't. Robert went past the sign, the boulder, and even the big tree. He crossed over a bridge, turned right at a mushroom patch, and walked right into a cave. When he walked into the cave, he fell and broke his arm. He managed to get back home, but he was in a lot of pain.

Robert had ignored his conscience. God has given you a conscience to help you know what is right and what is wrong. The Holy Spirit speaks to your conscience to help keep you out of trouble and protect you. But if you ignore the Holy Spirit, after a while you might try even more things you shouldn't. Robert stopped just past the tree the first time, but the next time he went all the way to the cave. Learn to listen to your conscience, because it can keep you from doing things you shouldn't. Robert got into trouble that he wouldn't have had to deal with had he listened to his conscience the first time. When you know something is wrong before you do it, be sure to do the right thing. But if you do make a mistake, turn around and do the right thing as soon as possible—before it's too late.

pray

Dear God, please help me to hear and follow the Holy Spirit as he speaks to my conscience.

"I knew I should have listened to that little voice inside!"

Secret Code

___ ___ ___ ___ ___   ___ ___   ___ ___ ___ ___ ___ ___   ___ ___
16 22 24 34 27   31 14   16 25 28 31 22 27   31 14

___ ___ ___ ___   ___ ___ ___ ___ ___ ___ ___ ___ ___ ___
39 14 29 34   11 14 27 28 11 25 22 27 11 22

A=24	G=33	M=23	S=28	Y=39
B=36	H=18	N=27	T=31	Z=21
C=11	I=25	O=14	U=29	
D=19	J=30	P=37	V=35	
E=22	K=26	Q=13	W=17	
F=15	L=16	R=34	X=38	

Unscramble These Words

niocncseec • raendg • taph • vcea • tneils • ubtorel • aimeskt • ainnwgr

Things to Do

- ☐ *If you aren't sure what the right thing to do is, ask God. Try also asking a parent or someone you trust if something is right or wrong.*
- ☐ *Write down what you think your conscience is telling you this week, whether or not you listened to it, and what happened as a result.*
- ☐ *Read Romans 14 and write down what you learned.*
- ☐ *Get a group of friends together and play the telephone game. At the end see how different the original message is from the finished message.*

do it

Things to Remember

wisdom

Because of this, I always try to maintain a clear conscience before God and all people.
— Acts 24:16

They demonstrate that God's law is written in their hearts, for their own conscience and thoughts either accuse them or tell them they are doing right. *— Romans 2:15*

If you have doubts about whether or not you should eat something, you are sinning if you go ahead and do it. . . . If you do anything you believe is not right, you are sinning. *— Romans 14:23*

Cling to your faith in Christ, and keep your conscience clear. For some people have deliberately violated their consciences; as a result, their faith has been shipwrecked. *— 1 Timothy 1:19*

When will our consciences grow so tender that we will act to prevent human misery rather than avenge it?
— Eleanor Roosevelt

Cowardice asks the question, "Is it safe?" Expediency asks the question, "Is it politic?" Vanity asks the question, "Is it popular?" But conscience asks the question, "Is it right?"
— Martin Luther King Jr.

The Yellow Brick Road

In *The Wizard of Oz* Dorothy ends up in the land of Oz because a tornado has carried her there like an airplane. At first, Dorothy is lost and confused, but there is hope, because she learns that all she has to do is follow the yellow brick road to the Emerald City so the wizard can help her get back to Kansas. Easy, right?

Wrong. On the yellow brick road, Dorothy meets several friends, but she also gets threatened by a mean green lady and chased around by a bunch of flying monkeys. So basically, Dorothy has the worst day of her life. Sure, she has her dog, a tin man, a scarecrow, and a lion to keep her company, but any day that includes a flying house, an angry woman meaner than your fourth-grade teacher, and King Kong's little brothers messing with you should be considered the worst day ever!

Life can often be like *The Wizard of Oz*. Movies and TV shows sometimes make it sound like life is going to be perfect, but in reality, life can be tough. Sometimes friends let you down. Sometimes parents leave and don't come back. Sometimes people you love die. Maybe you have a great life and maybe you don't, but either way, at some point life might not be perfect.

You have a road to walk in life, too. The Bible says that God has a plan for you and that "every moment" of your life "was laid out before a single day had passed" (Psalm 139:16). Maybe your road leads to becoming a fireman or hockey player or having a family someday. It's exciting to think about what you might be doing in ten years. You will make some good friends along the way, but other people might not like you. That's okay, because not everyone liked Jesus either. You may run into hard times and maybe even scary times, but it's okay because God is looking out for you. When you get disappointed, ask God for help, stick close to friends and family, and never give up.

pray

Dear God, please help me to keep going, even when the road is hard, and to remember that you are in control.

"I know you care. I just don't think anyone else does."

Secret Codes

```
A  B  C  D  E  F  G  H  I  J  K  L  M  N  O  P  Q  R  S  T  U  V  W  X  Y  Z
≈  ´  !  @  #  $  %  ^  &  *  (  )  "  Ï  =  +  Ω  ç  √  ∫  ∆  ©  ∂  ß  å  π
```

___ ___ ___ ___   ___ ___ ___   ___ ___ ___
 ∂   ^   #   Ï   å   =   ∆   %   #   ∫

___ ___ ___ ___ ___ ___ ___ ___ ___ ___ ___ ___
 @   &   √   ≈   +   +   =   &   Ï   ∫   #   @

___ ___ ___ ___ ___ ___ ___ ___ ___ ___ ___ ___ ___
 ≈   √   (%   =   @ $ =   ç   ^   #   )   +

Cross out the number of letters indicated and use the next letter to solve the secret code.

__ __   __ __ __ __   __ __ __   __ __

__ __ __ __   __ __ __   __ __

__ __ __ __ __ __

3, 2, 5, 3, 4, 6, 5, 2, 3, 4, 1, 5, 3, 5, 8, 7, 2, 6, 4, 5, 1, 3, 5

K Y T I K H N F T O K R R F A L E F W O J A H D E W O N L H N C G E I M G T
Y E C Y K H T E L L I H E D S W F L O Y E N B D F T C U T G E D W L O A J U I
P M C E N N F B L T F W D B E R D K U T Y E D K O O H U U M R G L I T E R H

"This sure isn't what I expected when I made the team . . ."

Things to Do

- ☐ *When you are feeling down, ask your dad or a friend to throw the football around with you.*
- ☐ *If you see someone else who is feeling down, try to lift up their spirits or simply listen to them if they want to talk about it.*
- ☐ *If you are really disappointed, try to visit a water park, because it's tough to be sad when you're having fun!*
- ☐ *Draw a picture of a flying monkey, cross it out, and hang it in your room. Remember that God is looking out for you.*

do it

wisdom

Things to Remember

This hope will not lead to disappointment. For we know how dearly God loves us, because he has given us the Holy Spirit to fill our hearts with his love. — *Romans 5:5*

"For I know the plans I have for you," says the LORD. "They are plans for good and not for disaster, to give you a future and a hope." — *Jeremiah 29:11*

David continued, "Be strong and courageous, and do the work. Don't be afraid or discouraged, for the LORD God, my God, is with you. He will not fail you or forsake you." — *1 Chronicles 28:20*

Why am I discouraged? Why is my heart so sad? I will put my hope in God! — *Psalm 42:11*

Endurance develops strength of character, and character strengthens our confident hope of salvation. — *Romans 5:4*

Accept finite disappointment, but never lose infinite hope.
— *Martin Luther King Jr.*

An adventure is only an inconvenience rightly considered. An inconvenience is only an adventure wrongly considered.
— *G. K. Chesterton*

Disappointment to a noble soul is what cold water is to burning metal; it strengthens, tempers, intensifies, but never destroys it.
— *Eliza Tabor*

Super Book

Tests can be tough. Math tests can be *really* tough. There are all sorts of tests in life. There are tests for school; there are things that test your friendships; and there are people who will try to test you and what you believe. Life is jammed full of tests, in fact. If two of your best friends get into an argument, what are you supposed to do? If your cousin tells you to steal the latest Star Wars collectible, what are you supposed to say?

In school, tests can be really tough, but tests in real life are sometimes even tougher. So how do you know what to do when you have to make a big decision? There is an answer to this question, and that answer is that you have to cheat. Yes, you read correctly. To face the tests in life you must cheat. But this doesn't mean that you peek at the brainy kid's answers in the middle of your science exam or that you try to change the rules during football practice. In fact, it is not okay to cheat anywhere else.

But in real-life tests, you are allowed to look at the answer key. Life is an open-book test, and the Bible is your answer key—your guide to know what to do and what not to do. So if your two friends are fighting and they both are at fault, the Bible says it's foolish to get involved in someone else's argument. Or when your cousin tries to get you to shoplift, the Ten Commandments say not to steal.

Some kids think that cheating in school or in sports is okay, but most cheaters eventually get caught, and then they get punished. But when you look to the Bible, you stay out of trouble. God gave you the Bible to help you make the best decisions in life. Many people today don't look to the Bible enough, but when you do, the tests of life don't seem as tough.

Dear God, thank you for giving me the Bible. Please help me as I read your Word to learn how to face my tests in life.

"I'm cheating on my life test."

Secret Codes

Add these numbers to solve the secret code.

15	11	11	17		8	10	18	10		12	16		12
+18	+3	+8	+11		+9	+4	+16	+9		+13	+12		+12

___ ___ ___ ___ ,   ___ ___ ___ ___   ___ ___   ___

8	13	10	22		12	9		13	14	15	17	11
+8	+11	+13	+15		+19	+5		+20	+15	+10	+2	+11

___ ___ ___ ___   ___ ___   ___ ___ ___ ___ ___

12	23		8	10		8	10
+11	+16		+7	+12		+14	+21

___ ___ , ___ ___ ___ ___

A=24	G=33	M=23	S=28	Y=39
B=36	H=18	N=27	T=31	Z=21
C=11	I=25	O=14	U=29	
D=19	J=30	P=37	V=35	
E=22	K=26	Q=13	W=17	
F=15	L=16	R=34	X=38	

Cross out every B, D, F, I, J, K, L, N, P, and W to solve the secret code.

KFDBMPWLJBDFIJOPNLBDFSWIFDBTPNLCHWNLKJ
IFDBPNLJKEBDFIAKFDBJTWPKJPNLKIEBDFIPWNL
RBDFIKSNPIFDBGFIJKLBDFIELPNTBDCIFDKLNPAW
PWWNKLUBDIWPNGBDFLHBDFIKLNPTDFIJKPNW

___ ___ ___ ___   ___ ___ ___ ___ ___ ___ ___

___ ___ ___   ___ ___ ___ ___ ___ ___

Things to Do

- Ask your parents or pastor what their favorite books of the Bible are and why. Read from these books at least twenty minutes each day and see how much you learn.
- Read Psalm 119 (you can read it in portions). Write your own poem about the Bible.
- Act out a Bible story with some friends and talk about what that story teaches.
- Find a Bible concordance (there might be one in the back of your Bible). The next time you are facing a test in life, look up what you are facing in the concordance to find help.

do it

wisdom

Things to Remember

These tablets were God's work; the words on them were written by God himself.
— *Exodus 32:16*

My word . . . will accomplish all I want it to, and it will prosper everywhere I send it.
— *Isaiah 55:10-11*

The seeds that fell on the good soil represent honest, good-hearted people who hear God's word, cling to it, and patiently produce a huge harvest. — *Luke 8:15*

Jesus replied, "My mother and my brothers are all those who hear God's word and obey it." — *Luke 8:21*

Don't just listen to God's word. You must do what it says. Otherwise, you are only fooling yourselves.
— *James 1:22*

Bible reading is an education in itself.
— *Alfred, Lord Tennyson*

When you read God's word, you must constantly be saying to yourself, "It is talking to me, and about me."
— *Søren Kierkegaard*

It is not at all incredible that a book which has been so long in the possession of mankind should contain many truths as yet undiscovered.
— *Bishop Butler*

Chalkboard Voices

read it

Do everything without complaining and arguing.
Philippians 2:14

Mrs. Dillard gave out homework on Friday. Her entire class complained but Mrs. Dillard gave it out anyhow. As she gave the assignments, the complaining got louder and louder. The class even said they wished they could have a different teacher, all because they didn't want homework over the weekend. Finally, Mrs. Dillard screeched her nails against the chalkboard in the front of the room. The ear-piercing noise got all the kids' attention as they covered their ears and flinched from the awful noise. Mrs. Dillard stopped and stood in front of the class, smiling. She seemed to have a change of heart because she told the class, "If you really want a different teacher, fine, but be careful what you ask for." The class left happy because they got no homework.

After the weekend all the kids came into class, sat at their desks, and waited for Mrs. Dillard to walk in. But she didn't. Instead, a 103-year-old angry lady walked in. This new teacher was really mean, and she gave out even *more* homework. They had homework Monday through Friday and were given twice as much homework for Saturday and Sunday! After just one week the kids began to ask when Mrs. Dillard would be back. When class was over and the kids left, the old lady sat down and took off her disguise, and Mrs. Dillard smiled.

Sometimes we don't appreciate what we have. The Israelites didn't either. They were God's chosen people. He delivered them from slavery and provided all their food and other needs, but they would often forget this and complain. God was not happy about this. Because of their complaining, they wandered around for forty years when they could've been relaxing in their new land. Jesus never promised us that life would be perfect, but the Bible does say we need to be thankful no matter what happens, and that means not complaining. Complaining tells God that what he's given you isn't good enough, that you know what you need better than he does. Complaining is like nails on a chalkboard to God.

pray

Dear God, I'm sorry for complaining. Please help me to be grateful for what I have. Thank you for always taking care of me.

If you can't say anything nice, don't say anything at all.

Crossword

ACROSS

2 The _____ says to be thankful, no matter what happens

7 Sometimes we don't _____ what we have

9 The Israelites _____ for forty years in the desert

10 People often _____ what God has done for them and complain

DOWN

1 The class covered their ears and _____ at the ear-piercing noise

3 The new teacher was really Mrs. _____

4 God delivered the Israelites from _____

5 _____ is like nails on a chalkboard to God

6 The new teacher gave _____ as much homework

8 Jesus never promised us that life would be _____

Things to Do

- [ ] *For the next week try not to complain at all, and take notice when something good happens.*
- [ ] *Read Numbers 11. Write down what the Israelites had to be thankful for and what they complained about.*
- [ ] *When you hear others complain, point out some things worth being thankful for.*
- [ ] *Make a list of things you've complained about recently. For each item on the list, write how you could have been thankful in that situation.*

do it

wisdom

Things to Remember

These people are grumblers and complainers, living only to satisfy their desires.
— Jude 1:16

Don't grumble as some of them did, and then were destroyed by the angel of death.
— 1 Corinthians 10:10

The LORD said to Moses, "I have heard the Israelites' complaints. Now tell them, 'In the evening you will have meat to eat, and in the morning you will have all the bread you want. Then you will know that I am the LORD your God.'"
— Exodus 16:11-12

I have learned the secret of living in every situation, whether it is with a full stomach or empty, with plenty or little. For I can do everything through Christ, who gives me strength. *— Philippians 4:12-13*

When any anxiety or gloom of the mind takes hold of you, make it a rule not to publish it by complaining; but exert yourselves to hide it, and by endeavoring to hide it you drive it away.
— Samuel Johnson

If you have time to whine and complain about something then you have the time to do something about it.
— Anthony J. D'Angelo

You can overcome anything if you don't bellyache.
— Bernard M. Baruch

To Boldly Go . . .

read it

Through their faith, the people in days of old earned a good reputation.

Hebrews 11:2

I n *Star Trek: Enterprise* there is a race of aliens called Andorians. These aliens are blue and have two antennas coming out of their heads. They look like a cross between Smurfs and insects. Andorians do not trust many people and have a major attitude toward Vulcans (the pointy-eared, elf-looking aliens, like Spock). The reason Andorians are grumpy and suspicious of everyone is they've been lied to a lot.

The Andorians and the Vulcans have a lot of arguments with each other, and the only man the Andorian leader will trust to help them is Captain Archer of the starship *Enterprise*. The Andorian leader trusts Archer and believes him to be a good and fair man. Because Captain Archer has proved himself to have integrity, he has built a good reputation, even with a grumpy blue guy who doesn't like humans. Captain Archer is able to work with both Vulcans and Andorians, avoiding a major war.

It's nice when people say great things about you, but what you're like inside is even more important. If people thought Captain Archer was a good person but he was really sneaky and lied a lot, his reputation wouldn't be earned and he wouldn't be able to stop a war. What is most important is that Captain Archer does the right thing by being fair, even when others aren't looking.

God doesn't want you to worry about your reputation. He wants you to worry about your character, the way you act whether others notice or not. The Pharisees of Jesus' time worried about their reputation, acting good on the outside, but inside they were mean. Jesus said that even though their reputation was good, God did not approve of their character. You should be more concerned about what God thinks of you than what other people think. You don't have to be a starship captain to build a good reputation; you just have to do the right thing at school, at church, and at home—and not just when others are watching. When you do that, God will take care of the rest.

Dear God, please help me to focus on doing right, whether others see it or not. I trust you for my reputation.

"I'm going crazy trying to please everyone!"

Word Search

REPUTATION CHARACTER ALIENS CONCERNED
TRUST ATTITUDE GRUMPY SUSPICIOUS ARGUMENTS
CAPTAIN FAIR INTEGRITY SNEAKY

R	B	D	K	U	T	D	E	N	R	E	C	N	O	C	L	A
S	E	T	G	E	S	G	P	C	D	B	G	Y	C	U	T	L
C	A	P	T	A	I	N	E	M	S	O	F	R	K	R	V	I
I	O	P	U	L	T	G	H	J	O	D	A	B	U	R	N	E
Y	T	A	T	T	I	T	U	D	E	J	I	D	I	M	R	N
P	U	W	C	H	A	R	A	C	T	E	R	V	D	N	P	S
V	G	V	W	Y	N	T	U	N	G	F	E	D	L	F	O	Y
B	J	G	T	P	H	F	I	R	Y	K	A	E	N	S	Y	E
V	J	T	P	L	E	T	G	O	F	X	V	L	R	U	W	Y
R	O	R	S	U	L	E	K	J	N	U	S	B	B	M	R	P
W	G	U	Q	A	O	A	R	G	U	M	E	N	T	S	Y	N
V	M	S	O	U	B	C	S	U	O	I	C	I	P	S	U	S
W	S	T	A	D	F	T	N	J	H	G	Y	T	U	R	W	D
K	F	J	I	N	T	E	G	R	I	T	Y	G	G	T	T	E

Secret Code

___ ___ ___   ___ ___ ___ ___ ___   ___ ___ ___ ___ ___
33 14 19   11 24 34 22 28   24 36 14 29 31

___ ___ ___ ___   ___ ___ ___ ___ ___ ___ ___ ___ ___
39 14 29 34   11 18 24 34 24 11 31 22 34

A=24   G=33   M=23   S=28   Y=39
B=36   H=18   N=27   T=31   Z=21
C=11   I=25   O=14   U=29
D=19   J=30   P=37   V=35
E=22   K=26   Q=13   W=17
F=15   L=16   R=34   X=38

Things to Do

- [ ] *Start building a strong reputation by listening to what your parents ask you to do. Get chores done and do your homework when you are supposed to and without being asked.*

- [ ] *Ask your teachers who they think is the best example of a man who had a great reputation for integrity. Find a book about this person and read more about him.*

- [ ] *Read Matthew 23, Jesus' critique of those who care more about reputation than character.*

- [ ] *This week, secretly do something nice for someone else and don't worry about being noticed for it.*

do it

wisdom

Things to Remember

Choose a good reputation over great riches; being held in high esteem is better than silver or gold. — *Proverbs 22:1*

A person who plans evil will get a reputation as a troublemaker. — *Proverbs 24:8*

A good reputation is more valuable than costly perfume. — *Ecclesiastes 7:1*

They were too good for this world, wandering over deserts and mountains, hiding in caves and holes in the ground. All these people earned a good reputation because of their faith. — *Hebrews 11:38-39*

When arguing with your neighbor, don't betray another person's secret. Others may accuse you of gossip, and you will never regain your good reputation. — *Proverbs 25:9-10*

Character is like a tree and reputation like a shadow. The shadow is what we think of it; the tree is the real thing.
— *Abraham Lincoln*

Be more concerned with your character than your reputation, because your character is what you really are, while your reputation is merely what others think you are.
— *John Wooden*

Safety Net Trapeze

read it

Hold on to the pattern of wholesome teaching you learned from me—a pattern shaped by the faith and love that you have in Christ Jesus.
2 Timothy 1:13

Humpty Dumpty was a very large egg man. He lived in a town with a lot of famous characters, like Mother Goose, Jack and the Giant, and even the Three Little Pigs. However, the pigs were not little at all; they just thought "The Three Little Pigs" looked better on their mailbox than "The Three Rather Large Hogs." Even though the town had lots of celebrities, there were still rules to be followed. For instance, you could not honk your horn within a hundred feet of the old lady who lived in a shoe, for fear it would wake up all her kids. Everyone knew that waking up *all* those kids meant trouble for the whole town.

For the most part everyone followed the rules, but Humpty Dumpty could not help himself from breaking the 17th rule of the town. That rule stated that no one could sit on the castle wall for fear of falling off it. But Dumpty just loved to watch the little town from the top of the wall while eating a peanut butter and jelly sandwich. But you probably already know what happened to good ol' Humpty. Humpty Dumpty fell off that high wall, and since he was an egg . . . well, it wasn't a pretty sight.

Rules are not made to be mean or to keep you

from having fun, but to keep you (and others) from getting into trouble. One of God's rules in the Bible is to not steal. This is a very good rule. It protects everyone, since while you might want to take what someone else has, you wouldn't like it if someone else took what was yours. Even though rules can be frustrating at times, they are there like a safety net to protect you and the others around you. The Bible says to obey the rules of the land, so God thinks even rules that aren't his are helpful. Had Humpty simply followed rule 17, he wouldn't have gotten hurt. Try your best to follow the rules so you don't end up like poor Humpty Dumpty.

Dear God, please help me to follow the rules, even when I don't understand them, knowing that rules are there for my protection.

Secret Code

Cross out the number of letters indicated and use the next letter to solve the secret code.

—— —— —— —— —— —— —— —— ——

—— —— —— —— —— —— ——

—— —— —— —— —— —— —— ——

—— —— —— —— ——

3, 2, 5, 3, 4, 6, 5, 2, 3, 4, 1, 5, 3, 5, 8, 7, 2, 6, 4, 5, 1, 6, 8, 4, 3, 2, 5, 7, 5

Y O M G N E E W S I N T Y U B I O T F E N V D W I K T T Y H
I P H H N H E O T E H R D U B A U B R E W C G I P M Y T J R
F H I O O H R E W G N U F J I P L F E W F M D O U K G R E D
L P K Y R L G R E I M O W W Y F E I U H I I Y H R F E K I N G E
U N G R D V R R B U U R F T B L P Y R E D V Y E U T V D W S

"But I have my diver's certificate. I'm sure that doesn't mean me."

NO DIVING!

120

Things to Do

- ☐ *Think up the rules you don't like and ask your parents what they are for. You might find out that some of those rules aren't so bad after all.*
- ☐ *Read Exodus 20, which provides God's list of rules, and write out why you think God made each one.*
- ☐ *Ask your principal for a copy of your school's code of conduct and read it to see how well you are following the rules of your school.*
- ☐ *Draw a map of a fantasy place where you will rule. Make a list of laws that you would make.*

do it

wisdom

Things to Remember

Learn to do good. Seek justice. Help the oppressed. Defend the cause of orphans. Fight for the rights of widows. — *Isaiah 1:17*

Everyone must submit to governing authorities. For all authority comes from God, and those in positions of authority have been placed there by God. — *Romans 13:1*

My children, listen when your father corrects you. Pay attention and learn good judgment.
— *Proverbs 4:1*

Respect everyone, and love your Christian brothers and sisters. Fear God, and respect the king.
— *1 Peter 2:17*

The LORD has told you what is good, and this is what he requires of you: to do what is right, to love mercy, and to walk humbly with your God. — *Micah 6:8*

The more I considered Christianity, the more I found that while it had established a rule and order, the chief aim of that order was to give room for good things to run wild.
— *G. K. Chesterton*

It's not wise to violate rules until you know how to observe them. — *T. S. Eliot*

If you work hard and play by the rules . . . you can achieve anything.
— *Arnold Schwarzenegger*

Mazed and Confused

read it

I am convinced that nothing can ever separate us from God's love. Neither death nor life, neither angels nor demons, neither our fears for today nor our worries about tomorrow—not even the powers of hell can separate us from God's love.
Romans 8:38

Chris loved the carnival! One of the new games at the carnival this year was the obstacle course. The obstacle course combined a maze, balance beams, and goofy mirrors. There were two courses. One was super easy, the other was much harder. Chris loved the carnival, but he wasn't very confident. He was nervous about trying anything new. He didn't think he was very good at very much, and he didn't want to mess up. So he chose the easier obstacle course. Chris made it through the easy course without any trouble, but he realized that only little kids picked the easy course. So even though he didn't mess up, he was embarrassed anyway.

People often do not value themselves the way God does. Chris was scared and insecure, so he always tried to pick easy things so he wouldn't mess up. Chris didn't realize how much God loved him, and he didn't realize he could've made it through the harder course with ease. God had given him talents and abilities and even a brain to figure things out. And even if Chris had messed up, God would've loved him anyway.

Lots of people are like Chris. They're insecure and don't realize their value. Having value means being worth something. A dollar bill can get you a pop, but a fifty-dollar bill can get you lots of pop. You have value, way more value in God's eyes than all the money in the world. You have so much value that God created you to be a unique, one-of-a-kind person. The Bible even says that "God showed his great love for us by sending Christ to die for us while we were still sinners" (Romans 5:8). You may not be the best at everything, but you don't have to be. Even if you make a mistake, you are still valuable to God. So don't be like Chris and always fear that you can't do things right. Take a chance from time to time. The easy route is not always the best one to take.

pray

Dear God, thank you for loving me, even if I mess up. Please help me to realize how valuable I am to you.

"It's a good thing God doesn't love me based on my grades."

Word Search

INSECURE VALUE CREATED CHANCE ABILITIES
TALENTS WORTH OBSTACLE MAZE MIRRORS
BEAM EMBARRASSED SCARED

V	M	F	O	U	R	C	B	M	K	L	E	P	I	O	R	P
D	B	D	K	U	T	I	E	A	E	P	T	U	E	B	L	M
S	U	T	G	E	S	N	P	Z	D	B	F	Y	C	S	T	Y
T	A	L	E	N	T	S	I	E	E	O	S	R	K	T	V	H
I	O	B	T	L	T	E	H	J	O	D	E	B	N	A	N	N
S	T	R	E	G	B	C	L	K	L	A	H	D	I	C	R	D
C	U	L	E	A	S	U	W	D	T	X	F	V	D	L	D	S
A	G	E	W	Y	M	R	U	E	V	A	L	U	E	E	O	H
R	J	C	T	P	H	E	D	R	M	T	D	U	O	O	Y	T
E	J	N	P	L	D	E	S	S	A	R	R	A	B	M	E	R
D	O	A	I	M	I	R	R	O	R	S	S	B	B	M	R	O
W	G	H	Q	B	O	F	J	R	Y	G	U	I	F	D	Y	W
W	S	C	A	D	A	B	I	L	I	T	I	E	S	R	W	D
K	F	J	G	U	T	F	D	G	J	F	H	G	G	T	T	E

Secret Code

A B C D E F G H I J K L M N O P Q R S T U V W X Y Z
≈ ´ ! @ # $ % ^ & * ( ) " Ï = + Ω ç √ ∫ ∆ © ∂ ß å π

___ ___ ___   ___ ___ ___   ___ ___ ___ ___ ___ ___
å = ∆   ≈ ç #   ≈) ∂ ≈ å √

___ ___ ___ ___ ___ ___ ___   ___ ___   ___ ___ ___
© ≈) ∆ ≈ ´) #   ∫ =   % = @

Things to Do

☐ *Write down what you think gives you value.*

☐ *Ask your parents what they love most about you. Tell them what you love most about them.*

☐ *Read Psalm 139. Write down how God has valued you.*

☐ *Make a list of things you think are valuable and research what they cost. Add up the totals, and think about how God values you more than all that combined!*

do it

Things to Remember

wisdom

The thief's purpose is to steal and kill and destroy. My purpose is to give . . . a rich and satisfying life. — *John 10:10*

The Father himself loves you dearly because you love me and believe that I came from God. — *John 16:27*

Since God chose you to be the holy people he loves, you must clothe yourselves with tenderhearted mercy, kindness, humility, gentleness, and patience. – *Colossians 3:12*

We know, dear brothers and sisters, that God loves you and has chosen you to be his own people. — *1 Thessalonians 1:4*

See how very much our Father loves us, for he calls us his children, and that is what we are! But the people who belong to this world don't recognize that we are God's children because they don't know him. — *1 John 3:1*

God is love. He didn't need us. But he wanted us. And that is the most amazing thing. — *Rick Warren*

Though our feelings come and go, God's love for us does not. — *C. S. Lewis*

God places the heaviest burden on those who can carry its weight. — *Reggie White*

A Snail Mystery

read it

For God loved the world so much that he gave his one and only Son, so that everyone who believes in him will not perish but have eternal life.
John 3:16

Batman is not the normal superhero. Most superheroes have superpowers. Batman uses his brain, money, and technology to give him an edge by making pretty cool weapons and cars. Batman lays down his life on a daily basis to help Gotham City, but given the choice, he would probably accept a superpower, like being able to fly or become invisible, to make his life a bit easier when fighting crime.

This is why Jesus is so amazing. First of all, Batman isn't real, but Jesus is. Jesus really *did* sacrifice his life to save your life. To really know how great a superhero Jesus is you must know about his sacrifices. He gave up a lot to help you and all humankind. Jesus willingly died so that you could spend eternity with God. Sin caused a great chasm between humanity and God, and the only way to bridge it was for Jesus to die. And he died a very painful death. The Romans put big spikes through his hands and feet and beat him up pretty badly. Because he died, you can now be friends with God if you accept Jesus as your Savior.

But some people don't realize what else he gave up. Jesus had it all nice up in heaven, but he chose to give up what he had to come to earth as a baby human. Batman would love to have superpowers, but Jesus "gave up his divine privileges" to save the world (Philippians 2:7). Even though Jesus was still God, he also chose to become human. For Jesus to become human would be like you transforming into a snail. Can you imagine how limiting it would be as a snail? Jesus was still able to heal and do super cool things, but he was also flesh and blood. He was still able to be put on a cross. Jesus not only died for you, but he also became like you to save you and save the day. Batman is cool, but Jesus is the real superhero.

pray

Dear God, thank you for sending Jesus to die for me so we could be friends. Jesus, thank you for your sacrifice.

"As much as I love you, I wouldn't die for you like Jesus did for me."

Secret Code

Cross out every D, F, G, I, K, L, N, P, Q, V, and Z to solve the secret code.

```
KLNQJDPVZEIKLSGQZVDFGULNKIGSDIKZPQV
CLQPVAFZNKLNQPMPQIGFEDKNQPTZVPIOG
IKLNQPVEVAZIKLNQPRTIGFDHQPNLKIAZVNQ
PSIKLAFGIKLPVBDGIKLNAZVPQNBFDKLGFDY
```

_ _ _ _ _   _ _ _ _   _ _

_ _ _ _ _   _ _   _   _ _ _ _

"Just think, Jesus did all that just for me..."

Things to Do

- ☐ *Thank God for allowing his Son to save you. Thank Jesus for his sacrifice in becoming like you and for his sacrifice on the cross.*
- ☐ *Go into the backyard or to a pet shop to look at some snails. Write about how tough it would be for you to become a snail.*
- ☐ *Read Philippians 2:5-11. Draw a picture of Jesus the superhero based on this passage.*
- ☐ *Tell five friends about what you have learned about Jesus' sacrifice in becoming a man.*

do it

Things to Remember

God presented Jesus as the sacrifice for sin. People are made right with God when they believe that Jesus sacrificed his life, shedding his blood. — *Romans 3:25*

Unlike those other high priests, he does not need to offer sacrifices every day. They did this for their own sins first and then for the sins of the people. But Jesus did this once for all when he offered himself as the sacrifice for the people's sins. — *Hebrews 7:27*

God's will was for us to be made holy by the sacrifice of the body of Jesus Christ, once for all time. — *Hebrews 10:10*

Now, most people would not be willing to die for an upright person, though someone might perhaps be willing to die for a person who is especially good. But God showed his great love for us by sending Christ to die for us while we were still sinners. — *Romans 5:7-8*

wisdom

If Jesus Christ be God and died for me, then no sacrifice can be too great for me to make for Him. — *C. T. Studd*

No man ever loved like Jesus. He taught the blind to see and the dumb to speak. He died on the cross to save us. He bore our sins. And now God says, "Because He did, I can forgive you." — *Billy Graham*

A King and His Horses

read it

But I confess my sins; I am deeply sorry for what I have done.
Psalm 38:18

There once lived a king who kept a herd of silver horses. These horses were the biggest and strongest horses ever to walk the earth. Everything in their lives was perfect. The king even let them march in special parades on holidays. The only rule was that none of them were allowed to walk into the green pool. If they did, the king would get rid of them. But a few of the silver horses walked through the green pool anyway. The horses got sick and turned green. Despite the sickness, anger, and conflict the green horses brought, they convinced the rest of the silver horses to go into the green pool too, until none of them were silver anymore. Many of the green horses became angry and refused to listen to anyone, but some of them were sad because they knew they had made a mistake. Those who admitted they shouldn't have disobeyed pleaded with the king to have mercy on them. And he did.

People are like these horses. When Adam and Eve disobeyed, all of creation went from being perfect to being flawed. God created a perfect place, but because of sin—the wrong things we do—nothing on earth is perfect now. Everyone is a sinner, even you, even the best person you can think of. Some people, like the angry horses, blame others and refuse any help. But other people, like the sad horses, realize they need God's help.

Sin separates us from God, but Jesus heals our relationship with God. Because Jesus lived a sinless life and died in our place for our sins, we can be God's friends. So if you ask Jesus to forgive you and confess him as Lord (admit that he's in charge), you can be reunited with God. This doesn't mean you will be perfect. You will still make mistakes from time to time, but when Jesus becomes your Lord, you will want to do what's right. And the good news is that even when we mess up, God will still have mercy on us.

Dear God, I'm so sorry for what I've done wrong. Please forgive me. Jesus, please be my Lord and show me how to do what is right.

"Being forgiven is like having a thousand pounds lifted off my back."

Crossword

ACROSS

3 _____ heals our relationship with God

6 Sin _____ us from God

9 _____ is a sinner

10 Jesus lived a _____ life

DOWN

1 We will still make _____ from time to time

2 Because of sin nothing is _____

4 We can be _____ with God

5 The horses marched in special _____

7 God _____ a perfect place

8 We must _____ Jesus as Lord

Things to Do

- [ ] Ask Jesus to forgive you of your sins and ask him to be the Lord of your life.
- [ ] Read John 3 in your Bible. Think about what it means to be "born again."
- [ ] Tell your friends about what Jesus has done for you personally and what he can do for them, too.
- [ ] Ask your pastor how he came to know Jesus.

do it

Things to Remember

My wounds fester and stink because of my foolish sins. — *Psalm 38:5*

An evil man is held captive by his own sins; they are ropes that catch and hold him.
— *Proverbs 5:22*

And forgive us our sins, as we have forgiven those who sin against us. — *Matthew 6:12*

For everyone has sinned; we all fall short of God's glorious standard. — *Romans 3:23*

If we claim we have no sin, we are only fooling ourselves and not living in the truth. But if we confess our sins to him, he is faithful and just to forgive us our sins and to cleanse us from all wickedness.
— *1 John 1:8-9*

wisdom

Sin is not hurtful because it is forbidden, but it is forbidden because it is hurtful.
— *Benjamin Franklin*

God had one son on earth without sin, but never one without suffering.
— *Saint Augustine*

Men are not punished for their sins, but by them.
— *Elbert Hubbard*

Samson and His Hair

Samson just might have been the strongest man to ever live. He took on whole armies by himself. If that's not impressive enough, he took on a whole army with his only weapon being a donkey's jawbone. However, just like Superman, he did have a weakness. The secret to his strength was the Nazirite vow his parents made to God before he was born that Samson's hair would never be cut. If his hair was cut, then his strength would fade away. Samson was a leader in his country and was stronger than anyone else, but his life was far from perfect.

In fact, things got really bad for Samson. His wife and father-in-law were killed. Later Samson even lost his great strength after his girlfriend tricked him. His eyes were poked out, and he was put in prison and forced to do hard labor. In the end, God helped Samson get revenge on his enemies, the Philistines, but it also cost Samson his life.

Life is tough. As you grow up you will realize that sometimes life is great and fun and totally exciting. But there are also times that are hard and sad. Many of the bad things that happened to Samson were his own fault, but other times they weren't. This is also true for you. If you disobey God or do something you know is wrong, that disobedience invites punishment. But sometimes bad things just happen.

God doesn't promise there won't be bad times, but he does promise that no matter what happens, he will always be with you. He also promises that he will never allow something to happen that's so bad you can't handle it. God has always been with you and has helped you get to where you are now, whether you've faced a lot of pain or not had much trouble yet. God's got your back. After Samson messed up, he asked God for help, and God helped him. In the toughest times it is most important to look to God for help.

pray

Dear God, thank you for always being with me. Whether life is hard or easy, please take care of me.

"God must think I'm pretty strong to be able to handle all this, huh?"

Secret Codes

Use the key to solve the secret code.

___ ___ ___ ___ ___ ___ ___ ___ : ___ ___ ___   ___ ___ ___
34 22 23 22 23 36 22 34   33 14 19   18 24 28

___ ___ ___ ___   ___ ___ ___ ___
39 14 29 34   36 24 11 26

A=24	G=33	M=23	S=28	Y=39
B=36	H=18	N=27	T=31	Z=21
C=11	I=25	O=14	U=29	
D=19	J=30	P=37	V=35	
E=22	K=26	Q=13	W=17	
F=15	L=16	R=34	X=38	

Cross out the number of letters indicated and use the next letter to solve the secret code.

___ ___ ___ ___   ___ ___   ___ ___ ___

___ ___   ___ ___ ___ ___ ___

___ ___ ___ ___ ___

3, 2, 5, 3, 4, 6, 5, 2, 3, 4, 1, 5, 3, 5, 8, 7, 2, 6, 4, 5, 1

PLULJHOYEDCGOPMGKDETITCSHOKGOTEWHIG
GKODRODGCDWIKNOKYRTTHTEOMBGTIULUTG
REDCGPIKYTEDHNGTLOYRGUIHREDMPITGVEYS

Things to Do

- ☐ Read the story of Samson in Judges 13–16. Write a short story about what might have happened to Samson if he had made better decisions.
- ☐ Talk to your parents about the lessons you could learn from Samson's life.
- ☐ Ask your pastor to tell you about a time when life got hard for him and what he did about it.
- ☐ Find and read the poem "Footprints in the Sand" and think of how Jesus has been with you in your life.

do it

wisdom

Things to Remember

You keep track of all my sorrows. You have collected all my tears in your bottle. You have recorded each one in your book. *– Psalm 56:8*

The temptations in your life are no different from what others experience. And God is faithful. He will not allow the temptation to be more than you can stand. When you are tempted, he will show you a way out so that you can endure. *– 1 Corinthians 10:13*

Sorrow is better than laughter, for sadness has a refining influence on us. *– Ecclesiastes 7:3*

I have told you all this so that you may have peace in me. Here on earth you will have many trials and sorrows. But take heart, because I have overcome the world. *– John 16:33*

Nearly all men can stand adversity, but if you want to test a man's character, give him power.
– Abraham Lincoln

Character cannot be developed in ease and quiet. Only through experience of trial and suffering can the soul be strengthened, ambition inspired, and success achieved.
– Helen Keller

Courage is not simply one of the virtues, but the form of every virtue at the testing point.
– C. S. Lewis

A Squid's Guide to What Not to Do

I trust in your unfailing love. I will rejoice because you have rescued me.

Psalm 13:5

Squidward is unlike many of the other characters on *SpongeBob SquarePants* because he seems to feel down a lot. While he is at work, he is *really* grumpy. The grumpier he gets, the more he doesn't want to be around anyone. SpongeBob and Patrick try to get Squidward to play with them, but most of the time Squidward slams the door in their faces. Other times he even throws things just to get rid of the sponge and starfish.

When things don't happen the way you want, it's easy to get disappointed. Squidward dreams of being a famous artist or musician, but he is stuck working at a fast-food joint instead. The problem is that Squidward handles his disappointments the wrong way. He shuts out his friends and hides inside his house. Even though he has friends who want to support him and hang out with him, he chooses to stay sad.

Life can be tough and it might not always go the way you want it to, but Squidward is the perfect example of what not to do. Shutting yourself inside and keeping things to yourself will only make things worse. God wants you to look to *him* for your happiness, not what is going right or wrong in your life. Circumstances are always changing. If you don't focus on God when things go well, you might forget to spend time with him when things go badly. And when things go badly and you don't focus on God, they will seem much worse.

Squidward ignores one of God's greatest gifts—friends. God is a good friend, the *best* friend. He wants to encourage you when you aren't feeling the greatest, but sometimes he does this through your other friends. When you are down, hanging with good friends is one of the best things to do. Friends can help you sort through problems and realize that even when life gets tough, you have God and good friends on your side. When you feel like Squidward, open up to God and let your friends help you. You'll be glad you did.

pray

Dear God, thank you for my friends who encourage me when I'm down. Please help me do the same for them when they need it.

"I always feel better when I'm with these guys."

Word Search

Find the words from the story in the box below.

HAPPINESS FOCUS FRIENDS HANGING CHANGING
PROBLEMS FORGET DISAPPOINTMENTS HIDES
SUPPORT CHOOSES DOWN RIGHT WRONG

T	E	G	R	O	F	I	E	A	E	P	T	U	E	J	L	M
S	U	T	G	E	O	G	P	C	D	B	D	Y	C	U	T	Y
G	S	N	O	I	C	W	I	U	E	O	S	L	P	R	V	H
I	U	C	T	L	U	G	H	J	W	D	V	B	R	S	N	A
Y	P	H	F	G	S	O	L	N	L	J	H	D	O	E	R	N
P	P	A	E	W	S	J	S	D	U	X	F	V	B	S	D	G
G	O	N	H	A	P	P	I	N	E	S	S	D	L	O	O	I
N	R	G	T	P	H	F	D	R	M	T	D	U	E	O	Y	N
O	T	I	P	T	H	G	I	R	F	H	V	L	M	H	W	G
R	O	N	I	U	L	E	K	J	T	U	I	B	S	C	R	P
W	G	G	Q	B	O	F	J	R	Y	G	U	D	F	D	Y	N
V	M	F	S	D	N	E	I	R	F	L	E	P	E	O	R	P
D	I	S	A	P	P	O	I	N	T	M	E	N	T	S	W	D
K	F	J	G	U	T	F	D	G	J	F	H	G	G	T	T	E

"It's a lot easier to rely on God when things are going badly."

Things to Do

- ☐ *Ask God to help you to be more thankful for your friends.*
- ☐ *Write God a note and thank him for being your best friend.*
- ☐ *When you are feeling down, spend some time with your friends. If one of your friends is going through a rough time, try going over to his house to cheer him up.*

do it

Things to Remember

Don't worry about anything; instead, pray about everything. Tell God what you need, and thank him for all he has done.
— *Philippians 4:6*

I pray that God, the source of hope, will fill you completely with joy and peace because you trust in him. Then you will overflow with confident hope through the power of the Holy Spirit. — *Romans 15:13*

For if we are faithful to the end, trusting God just as firmly as when we first believed, we will share in all that belongs to Christ. — *Hebrews 3:14*

But let all who take refuge in you rejoice; let them sing joyful praises forever. Spread your protection over them, that all who love your name may be filled with joy. — *Psalm 5:11*

Save me so I can praise you publicly at Jerusalem's gates, so I can rejoice that you have rescued me. — *Psalm 9:14*

wisdom

Never, never, never give up!
— *Winston Churchill*

Why do we fall, sir? So we can get back up again. — *Alfred in Batman Begins*

Obstacles don't have to stop you. If you run into a wall, don't turn around and give up. Figure out how to climb it, go through it, or work around it.
— *Michael Jordan*

Building Tree Houses

Have you forgotten the encouraging words God spoke to you as his children? He said, "My child, don't make light of the LORD's discipline, and don't give up when he corrects you. For the LORD disciplines those he loves, and he punishes each one he accepts as his child."

Hebrews 12:5-6

Sometimes guys think love is mushy and gushy and has something to do with Mom pinching their cheeks and messing up their hair. But people only know about true love by seeing God's example and by reading the Bible. Love is actually pretty cool.

God loves you so much that he allowed his only Son to die so you can be with him in heaven. God loves you so much that he also gave you talents and people who care about you.

There is another part of God's love, though, that is often more painful for the moment, but better in the long run. It's kind of like when your parents ground you for cheating on your homework. They ground you so you know how important it is to do things the right way and learn important information that you will need as you get older.

Think of life as a tree house. If you rush through the work, cut corners, and are not careful, you may build a shaky house that might just fall out of the tree. It takes patience and hard work, as well as time, to make a tree house that's safe. God tries to keep his people from getting into big messes, but sometimes people ignore God and do things their own way. God loves you so much that he would rather discipline you and help you grow stronger and more mature than keep consequences away and have you never learn.

How does God show his love this way? One of the biggest ways is through your parents, teachers, and pastors. Those people are looking out for you and want what's best for you. But this often means making sure you know right from wrong, and that means handing out consequences. God isn't a mean old guy just waiting to pounce on you the moment you make a mistake. He loves you and wants to help you, even when it's painful at the time. Discipline may not be the most fun thing ever, but be honest—it's better than getting your cheeks pinched.

pray

Dear God, thank you for loving me. Please help me understand your disciplining love better.

"I know it's for my own good. I just wish it didn't hurt so much."

Unscramble These Words

nispicdlie • trnseap • rhesctae • spsatro • vleo • rtauem • eeahvn • neastlt • hnipcde

Secret Code

6	6	16	11	14	14
+12	+8	+11	+11	+14	+17

___ ___ ___ ___ ___ ___

13	14	6	3	9	24	10	12	8	16		14	15		16
+6	+11	+22	+8	+16	+13	+6	+13	+19	+6		+11	+13		+8

___ ___ ___ ___ ___ ___ ___ ___ ___ ___   ___ ___   ___

12	3	12	15		9	7		10	7	16	16
+3	+11	+22	+8		+5	+8		+6	+7	+19	+6

___ ___ ___ ___   ___ ___   ___ ___ ___ ___

A=24 G=33 M=23 S=28 Y=39
B=36 H=18 N=27 T=31 Z=21
C=11 I=25 O=14 U=29
D=19 J=30 P=37 V=35
E=22 K=26 Q=13 W=17
F=15 L=16 R=34 X=38

"If it hurts you more than it hurts me, why can't I ground you for a week?"

144

Things to Do

- ☐ Ask your parents to describe a time when they feel God helped them by disciplining them.
- ☐ Thank God and your parents for their loving discipline, even when you don't understand it.
- ☐ Make a list of your last few punishments, along with what you did to deserve them. Look at each and think how it was motivated by love.
- ☐ Write a song about the good benefits that come from God's discipline.

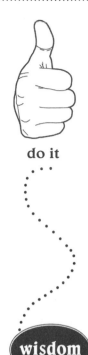

do it

Things to Remember

God's way is perfect. All the LORD's promises prove true. He is a shield for all who look to him for protection. *— Psalm 18:30*

Give thanks to the God of gods. His faithful love endures forever. *— Psalm 136:2*

For the law was given through Moses, but God's unfailing love and faithfulness came through Jesus Christ. *— John 1:17*

And may you have the power to understand, as all God's people should, how wide, how long, how high, and how deep his love is. *— Ephesians 3:18*

Love does no wrong to others, so love fulfills the requirements of God's law. *— Romans 13:10*

wisdom

God loves you just the way you are, but he refuses to leave you that way. He wants you to be just like Jesus.
— Max Lucado

God loves each of us as if there were only one of us.
— Saint Augustine

Let God's promises shine on your problems.
— Corrie ten Boom

Reach for the Stars

What do you think of when you think of heaven? Some people think of heaven as only a big, blue place with clouds and harps and nothing else. But that isn't true. Heaven is far cooler than that.

God has made everything beautiful for its own time. He has planted eternity in the human heart, but even so, people cannot see the whole scope of God's work from beginning to end.
Ecclesiastes 3:11

Everything dies at some point. Trees die, dogs die, even people die. Most of the time people look at death as a sad thing, but if someone knows Jesus, death is really the beginning of a much nicer life. When a person dies, there are two destinations. The bad place is hell. The good place is heaven.

Imagine the most amazing day—playing baseball, or skateboarding, or playing video games with all your best friends—and heaven is better than that. Imagine the best food, because the Bible talks about a huge feast! Think of all the fun you've had in your life and times that by a hundred, and you still don't even get *close* to how awesome heaven is going to be! Not only is heaven full of cool things, but it is also full of great people. There are lots of people you know about who will be there. Some of your friends and family members will be there, and many of the people you read about in the Bible will be, too. But the best part is that Jesus will be there. Yes, you will actually be able to hang out with Jesus!

Sometimes people forget how amazing heaven is really going to be. Everyone who trusts in Jesus will be in heaven, and they will no longer worry about crying or pain. No one will think about the bad things they went through here on earth. Think of the best place on earth, and it doesn't even come close to heaven. Think about it. How many places do you know that have streets made out of *gold*! But what makes heaven truly amazing is that you will be in God's presence everywhere—forever! Remember that no matter what happens here on earth, good or bad, heaven is where you will spend eternity if you trust in Jesus.

pray

Dear God, thank you for the hope of heaven. Please help me live my life now in a way worthy of heaven.

"This is great, but heaven's going to be even better!"

Secret Codes

Cross out every B, D, F, G, J, K, Q, T, U, and Z to solve the secret code.

KBQBHDKZUEGFDBJZAKTUKQVGFEBNDFGDJT
QITUSFDBGZQTAUDKZRJGKQETZZBDAFGJLLQ
DUDBZGGFFDBDYZKKQATUDWZKGEUKJGSFDB
ZTUZOKJGMFQTUEZBPDJKLQTAZBDFJCGKQTE

— — — — — — — — —

— — — — — — — — — — — — —

— — — — —

Use the key to solve the secret code.

— — —   — — — —   — — — —   — — — — —
39 14 29   17 25 16 16   23 22 22 31   30 22 28 29 28

— — — —   — —   — — — —   — —
15 24 11 22   31 14   15 24 11 22   25 27

— — — — — —
18 22 24 35 22 27

A=24 G=33 M=23 S=28 Y=39
B=36 H=18 N=27 T=31 Z=21
C=11 I=25 O=14 U=29
D=19 J=30 P=37 V=35
E=22 K=26 Q=13 W=17
F=15 L=16 R=34 X=38

"I really miss my grandpa. I can't wait to see him in heaven."

Things to Do

- ☐ *If you haven't already done so, pray and ask Jesus to forgive you of your sins and to be the Lord of your life.*
- ☐ *Write down any questions you have about heaven and ask your pastor.*
- ☐ *Ask your friends what aspect of heaven they are most excited about.*
- ☐ *Draw a picture of what you think heaven will be like.*

do it

Things to Remember

God blesses those who are poor and realize their need for him, for the Kingdom of Heaven is theirs. — *Matthew 5:3*

The Kingdom of God is not a matter of what we eat or drink, but of living a life of goodness and peace and joy in the Holy Spirit. — *Romans 14:17*

Store your treasures in heaven, where moths and rust cannot destroy, and thieves do not break in and steal. — *Matthew 6:20*

I heard a loud shout from the throne, saying, "Look, God's home is now among his people! He will live with them, and they will be his people. God himself will be with them. He will wipe every tear from their eyes, and there will be no more death or sorrow or crying or pain. All these things are gone forever." — *Revelation 21:3-4*

Go and announce to them that the Kingdom of Heaven is near. — *Matthew 10:7*

wisdom

Heaven—the treasury of everlasting life. — *William Shakespeare*

Earth has no sorrow that heaven cannot heal. — *Thomas Moore*

But all endings are also beginnings. We just don't know it at the time. — *Mitch Albom*

The Clown and the Cowboy

*For the word of the
LORD holds true,
and we can trust
everything he does.*
Psalm 33:4

A clown and a cowboy went rock climbing. They climbed a massive mountain in the middle of the wilderness with no one else around. They were both having fun until the cowboy got stuck on one of the cliffs. He called up to the clown for help. The clown, knowing the cowboy needed something to grab on to, tossed down a rope to the cowboy.

Right before the cowboy was about to grab the rope, he noticed it was frayed in the middle. The cowboy yelled, "I can't grab this rope! It'll break and I'll fall!" The clown chuckled. "I know, but I thought it was a funny joke." The cowboy wasn't laughing. The clown threw something else down, but the cowboy saw it was a snake and said, "I can't grab on to this snake—it might bite me!" The clown laughed and then he threw another rope down, but it was covered with thorns. The cowboy was again upset at the clown, but the clown said he was just trying to have some fun. The clown knew it was time to really help the cowboy, so he threw down a big, strong rope, but the cowboy wouldn't grab it. The cowboy said, "What's wrong with this one? I don't trust you anymore." The clown tried to convince him that this rope was good and that he was done joking, but the cowboy didn't believe him. So they stayed there on that cliff and are still there today, all because the cowboy doesn't trust the clown.

Trust is a hard thing to earn, and it is even harder to get back if you break it. God wants you to trust him, and he wants others to be able to trust you. If you say you're going to do something, make sure you do it. Keep your promises and help people when they need it. You are a living example of God to other people, so if they can't trust you, they might find it hard to trust God. Don't be a clown. Be someone people can trust.

pray

Dear God, please help me to trust you more and to be trustworthy so that others will trust you, too.

"I trust you and I trust me . . . but sometimes I'm not sure about you."

Word Search

TRUST HELP JOKING PROMISES CONVINCE
CLIFF COWBOY CLOWN FRAYED BREAK
CHUCKLED TOSSED SNAKE THORNS

```
D B D S E S I M O R P T U E J L M
S U T C H U C K L E D F Y C U T Y
F R A Y E D W I U V O S L K K V H
I O P T L T G H E L P V B C A N N
Y T R R G B O L K L J H O I E R D
P O W U W S J W D U X W V D R D S
V S V S Y N R O N G B E D L B O R
B S G T P N F D K O T D S O O Y E
V E U P L E W G Y I X V N R U W Y
R D P I U L E O J T N S R B M R C
W G F Q B O F J L Y G G O F D Y L
V M E C N I V N O C L E H I O R I
W S Q A D F K N J H G Y T U R W F
K E K A N S F D G J F H G G T T F
```

Secret Code

A B C D E F G H I J K L M N O P Q R S T U V W X Y Z
≈ ´ ! @ # $ % ^ & * ( ) " Ï Ç + Ω ç √ ∫ ∆ © ç √ ∫ å π

___ ___ ___   ___ ___ ___ ___ ___   ___ ___ ___   ___ ___
 %   Ç   @   ∂   ≈   Ï   ∫   √   å   Ç   ∆   ∫   Ç

___ ___ ___ ___ ___   ___ ___ ___   ___ ___ ___
 ∫   ç   ∆   √   ∫   ^   &   "   ≈   Ï   @

___ ___ ___ ___ ___ ___   ___ ___   ___ ___ ___ ___ ___   ___ ___ ___
 Ç   ∫   ^   #   ç   √   ∫   Ç   ∫   ç   ∆   √   ∫   å   Ç   ∆

Things to Do

- [ ] *Don't make promises you can't keep. If you make a promise, do your best to keep it.*
- [ ] *Think about people you trust and people you don't trust and what characteristics make them different. Try to practice what distinguishes those you trust.*
- [ ] *Ask your parents the best ways to earn others' trust.*
- [ ] *Write a short skit about the importance of trust.*

do it

Things to Remember

Many sorrows come to the wicked, but unfailing love surrounds those who trust the LORD. — *Psalm 32:10*

In him our hearts rejoice, for we trust in his holy name. — *Psalm 33:21*

Just say a simple, "Yes, I will," or "No, I won't." Anything beyond this is from the evil one.
— *Matthew 5:37*

If you are untrustworthy about worldly wealth, who will trust you with the true riches of heaven? And if you are not faithful with other people's things, why should you be trusted with things of your own? — *Luke 16:11-12*

The Lord replied, "A faithful, sensible servant is one to whom the master can give the responsibility of managing his other household servants and feeding them." — *Luke 12:42*

wisdom

Trust men and they will be true to you; treat them greatly, and they will show themselves great.
— *Ralph Waldo Emerson*

Your faithfulness makes you trustworthy to God.
— *Edwin Louis Cole*

To be trusted is a greater compliment than being loved.
— *George MacDonald*

War of the Worlds

He chose to give birth to us by giving us his true word. And we, out of all creation, became his prized possession.

James 1:18

In the movie *War of the Worlds*, Tom Cruise fights to keep his family safe from invading aliens. The movie was popular, but *War of the Worlds* has also been a book and a radio show. In fact, when this story was acted out over the radio in 1938, some people thought it was real. A radio had no pictures, so they thought the events acted out with voices and sound effects were a real-life newscast. Many of those who heard the broadcast hid in fear to protect themselves from the big, bad aliens. They didn't know that the show was just a story written by H. G. Wells.

The radio played a big part in people's lives back then. Today, computers, TVs, and iPods are used by millions of people every day. All these forms of media are important in telling you and your parents what is going on in the world. If there is a tornado coming near you, your dad can hear about it on TV or the Internet or by getting a text on his phone. If you are feeling down and want to feel better, you might listen to an encouraging song on your iPod. Art and media are probably a large part of your life. The problem is that these things don't always speak the truth. Many songs, TV shows, and even the news can tell a story in a way that is not totally honest.

Media and art are very powerful ways of communicating to people, but if you don't have a solid understanding of who God is and what he wants, media and art can also start to make you think things you shouldn't. If your favorite TV character says it's okay to lie to your parents, but you know God wouldn't like that, you should think twice about whether what you're watching or listening to is really good for you. Media and art have a tremendous power to influence people, but you have the power to decide to switch them on or off.

Dear God, please give me wisdom to choose what to watch, listen to, and believe, and the strength to turn off what I shouldn't.

"I really like that song—it's just the words that are disturbing."

Crossword

ACROSS

5 The media can tell a story in a way that is not _____

6 *War of the Worlds* was originally acted out on the _____

7 Media and art are powerful ways of _____

8 Media and art have a tremendous power to _____

9 You should think twice about whether what you're watching is really _____ for you

DOWN

1 TV shows, movies, and news are all part of the _____

2 When *War of the Worlds* was first played, people thought it was a real-life _____

3 If you're feeling down, you can listen to an _____ song

4 *War of the Worlds* talked about _____ invading

"I don't understand how the same story can sound so different on two different networks."

Things to Do

- ☐ *Make a list of your favorite TV shows and songs. Write down what messages are behind the shows and songs.*
- ☐ *Talk to your parents about what they think is good and bad to listen to.*
- ☐ *Try turning off the TV, computer, iPod, and video games for a few hours this week to help you hear God better.*
- ☐ *Keep a log of the time you spend this week with TV, video games, the Internet, music, etc. Discuss with your parents, pastor, or friends how you spend your time.*

do it

Things to Remember

wisdom

Guard your heart above all else, for it determines the course of your life.
— Proverbs 4:23

Tune your ears to wisdom, and concentrate on understanding. *— Proverbs 2:2*

Fix your thoughts on what is true, and honorable, and right, and pure, and lovely, and admirable. Think about things that are excellent and worthy of praise. *— Philippians 4:8*

Turn my eyes from worthless things, and give me life through your word. *— Psalm 119:37*

Let every created thing give praise to the LORD, for he issued his command, and they came into being.
— Psalm 148:5

A picture is worth a thousand words.
— Napoleon Bonaparte

Art is a collaboration between God and the artist, and the less the artist does the better. *— Andre Gide*

Art, like morality, consists of drawing the line somewhere.
— G. K. Chesterton

Wild Wild West

Happy are those who hear the joyful call to worship, for they will walk in the light of your presence, LORD.

Psalm 89:15

I n the old days, the West was almost mythical. There were great battles and good guys and bad guys, but over time, as real-life events got retold over and over, the stories got bigger and scarier. At first, West Willie fought one guy and protected a lady. But the story was told so many times, with people changing the details a little at a time, that it wasn't too long before it left out the lady's being saved altogether. It became a story about how West Willie fought off 103 bad guys and saved the entire universe!

Sometimes people forget the truth. For Christians the Bible is the absolute truth for everyone to follow, but people can misrepresent or forget the truths inside the Bible. For example, what do you think of when you hear the word "worship"? Some might picture the music part of a church service. For many Christians, worship has become simply that. But that is not the only form of worship mentioned in the Bible. The truth is that worship has more to do with attitude. It's when you're thankful and respectful toward God. You can worship God while doing nearly anything—drawing, playing sports, or even doing your chores. God loves it when you worship him in everything you do. If you do your homework with a thankful attitude, God loves that. An important way to worship God is with your giving. You can give money to the poor or give your time to help your grandparents by mowing their lawn.

Worship was never meant to be only at church. Why don't people worship God in all they do? Most of the time people just forget because they get so busy. When you have to do the dishes, take out the trash, mow the lawn, and vacuum the living room all in one hour, it's easy to think only about all the things you have to do rather than worshiping God while you do them. But God ultimately calls us to be "a living and holy sacrifice" (Romans 12:1), worshiping him in all we do.

pray

Dear God, please help me remember to worship you and be thankful in all I do.

"God is so cool to have made all this!"

Secret Code

27	6	18		7	14	14		6	9	21	9	12	14	15
+12	+8	+11		+4	+10	+13		+11	+5	+13	+19	+6	+11	+22
___	___	___		___	___	___		___	___	___	___	___	___	___

13	12	6		16	11	26	10	9	8	16	11
+20	+2	+13		+8	+16	+13	+7	+9	+14	+18	+11
___	___	___		___	___	___	___	___	___	___	___

A=24	G=33	M=23	S=28	Y=39
B=36	H=18	N=27	T=31	Z=21
C=11	I=25	O=14	U=29	
D=19	J=30	P=37	V=35	
E=22	K=26	Q=13	W=17	
F=15	L=16	R=34	X=38	

"I never knew worshiping God on a fishing trip could be so rewarding!"

Things to Do

- [ ] *When you do your homework, do your best and be sure to thank God for all that he has done for you.*
- [ ] *Read Psalm 95. Then talk to your parents about what they think makes a good worshiper.*
- [ ] *The next time you laugh, stop and tell God how thankful you are for him.*
- [ ] *Make a list of ways you spend your time. Then think of specific ways that these activities can be worship.*

do it

Things to Remember

Come, let us worship and bow down. Let us kneel before the LORD our maker.
— Psalm 95:6

Worship the LORD in all his holy splendor. Let all the earth tremble before him.
— Psalm 96:9

Worship the LORD with gladness. Come before him, singing with joy. *— Psalm 100:2*

The time is coming—indeed it's here now—when true worshipers will worship the Father in spirit and in truth. The Father is looking for those who will worship him that way. *— John 4:23*

Exult in his holy name; rejoice, you who worship the LORD. *— Psalm 105:3*

wisdom

I think worship is a lifestyle, first of all.
— Michael W. Smith

Everyone ought to worship God according to his own inclinations, and not to be constrained by force.
— Flavius Josephus

We only learn to behave ourselves in the presence of God.
— C. S. Lewis

Video Game Champions

Madden Football is one of the most popular video games on the planet. Colleges across the country hold Madden Football tournaments, and this video game even has a TV show based on people who compete against each other in Madden Football. To be good at a game like Madden, you have to learn how to win and also learn how not to lose. If you never learn, then you will likely make the same mistakes over and over again. If you play Wii Bowling and always aim for the gutter, you will nearly always throw the ball in the gutter.

Learning is important if you want to be good at video games. Learning is also important in real life. For example, it is important to learn that eating volcanic-hot BBQ sauce with jalapeño and chili peppers might not be the best idea unless you don't mind burning your mouth off. There are different ways to learn. One is by learning from your mistakes. When you mess up, take notice and try not to mess up again. Another is to learn from other people's mistakes. If you see Todd toss his cell phone to Michael but it falls and breaks, you can see that you shouldn't toss cell phones. But watching other people make mistakes isn't the only way to learn from them. You can also ask about mistakes others have made so you can avoid them yourself.

God has placed people in your life to help you know what to do. He knew you'd need help. The Bible says to obey your parents and to listen to people who know more than you do. Proverbs 13:18 points out that those who accept correction will be honored, but those who don't will end in disgrace. The truth is, those older than you have probably already experienced some of what you're going through and can help you not to make the same mistakes they did. God gave you people to learn from. It's your job to be willing to learn from people wiser than yourself.

Dear God, please help me to be willing to learn from my mistakes and the experiences of others.

"I like learning from other people's mistakes better than learning from my own!"

Secret Codes

Use the key to solve the secret code.

A B C D E F G H I J K L M N O P Q R S T U V W X Y Z
≈ ´ ! @ # $ % ^ & * ( ) " Ï = + Ω ç √ ∫ Δ © ∂ ß å π

___ ___ ___ ___ ___ ___ ___ ___ ___ ___ ___ ___
) # ≈ ç Ï $ ç = " ∫ ^ #

___ ___ ___ ___ ___ ___ ___ ___ ___ ___ ___ ___
+ # = +) # ≈ ç = Δ Ï @

___ ___ ___
å = Δ

Cross out the number of letters indicated and use the next letter to solve the secret code.

___ ___ ___ ___ ___ ___ ___ ___ ___ ___

___ ___ ___ ___ ___ ___ ___ ___

___ ___ ___

3, 2, 5, 3, 4, 6, 5, 2, 3, 4, 1, 8, 5, 3, 5, 8, 7, 2, 6, 4, 5, 6, 7, 4

Y H F G L K O W J Y R C D P U B K Y F E W N K H Y E D G E
U J H B N W P I Y H F S O Y G V E U N W Y U J V F I G R O J F
E R I U M V T E D J U F L N D W R I K N D T C N U H R D W E
E O R F E E G R E O L D H J E U Y D H J Y R E J I Y E L O Y L P

"If those who accept correction are wise, I'll be up there with Solomon!"

Things to Do

- [ ] *Make a list of the people you respect most. Ask those people to tell you the best lesson they've learned, and then try to practice it yourself.*
- [ ] *Don't watch more than an hour of TV each day this week. Instead, read a book that teaches you something important.*
- [ ] *Learn the Ten Commandments in Exodus 20:2-17. Memorize all of them.*
- [ ] *Talk to those who are younger than you and share the lessons you've learned in your life.*

do it

wisdom

Things to Remember

As I learn your righteous regulations, I will thank you by living as I should! – *Psalm 119:7*

You offer forgiveness, that we might learn to fear you. – *Psalm 130:4*

What you learn from them will crown you with grace and be a chain of honor around your neck. – *Proverbs 1:9*

These things happened to them as examples for us. They were written down to warn us who live at the end of the age. – *1 Corinthians 10:11*

Instruct the wise, and they will be even wiser. Teach the righteous, and they will learn even more.
– *Proverbs 9:9*

I am always ready to learn although I do not always like being taught.
– *Winston Churchill*

Anyone who stops learning is old, whether at twenty or eighty. – *Henry Ford*

Learn from yesterday, live for today, hope for tomorrow.
– *Albert Einstein*

Swimming Pals

read it

Accept other believers who are weak in faith, and don't argue with them about what they think is right or wrong.
Romans 14:1

Butch and Cassidy were best of friends. They played and laughed together. They even went swimming together almost every day in the summer. If Butch was sad, Cassidy would make him laugh, and if Cassidy was grouchy, Butch would do his SpongeBob SquarePants impersonation to cheer him up. They were the coolest, closest, best buddies ever—until one day Butch said something that really made Cassidy mad. Then Cassidy said something to Butch that made Butch madder than Cassidy. So they stopped talking to each other.

They didn't hang out anymore and even tried hard not to look at each other at school or church. They didn't talk for a whole week. Then a week turned into a month, and a month turned into a year. As time passed, both of them would not let the conflict go. Both of them grew up, got married, and had kids, and their kids had kids, and before they knew it, they were both old men.

One day Butch decided to go to the lake where he and Cassidy used to swim. He found a log, sat down, and looked at the water. He heard a noise, so he turned his head and saw Cassidy sitting a few feet away. The two old men wanted to argue and tell each other off, but then they both realized something:

Neither of them could remember what had started their fight when they were kids. They had been so busy holding a grudge that neither of them took time to try and make things right.

If you get into a disagreement with a friend, do your best to make things right. If you messed up, apologize. If your friend messed up, forgive him. God forgave you, so you should forgive others. Friendship is way too important to let something that won't be important in fifty years mess that up. Butch and Cassidy could have been friends their whole lives, but they let something small get in the way. And it was hard for them to be swimming pals at 87.

"I know I'm mad at you! I just can't remember why."

Word Search

FRIEND APOLOGIZE FORGIVE SWIM FIGHT GRUDGE
ARGUE CONFLICT DISAGREEMENT IMPERSONATION YEARS

D	B	D	K	U	T	E	Z	I	G	O	L	O	P	A	I	M
S	C	T	G	E	S	G	P	C	D	B	F	Y	C	U	M	Y
G	V	O	O	F	E	W	I	E	U	G	R	A	K	R	P	H
I	O	P	N	L	R	G	H	J	O	D	F	B	N	S	E	N
Y	T	R	F	F	B	I	L	K	L	J	O	D	I	R	R	D
P	U	W	E	W	L	J	E	D	U	X	R	V	D	A	S	E
V	S	V	W	Y	N	I	U	N	G	F	G	D	L	E	O	G
B	J	W	T	P	H	F	C	R	D	T	I	U	O	Y	N	D
V	J	U	I	L	E	T	G	T	F	X	V	L	R	U	A	U
R	O	P	I	M	L	E	K	J	T	U	E	B	B	M	T	R
W	G	F	Q	B	F	I	G	H	T	G	U	I	F	D	I	G
D	I	S	A	G	R	E	E	M	E	N	T	P	I	O	O	P
W	S	Q	A	D	F	K	N	J	H	G	Y	T	U	R	N	D
K	F	J	G	U	T	F	D	G	J	F	H	G	G	T	T	E

Secret Code

___ ___   ___ ___ ___ ___   ___ ___ ___ ___   ___ ___   ___ ___ ___ ___
19 14   39 14 29 34   36 22 28 31   31 14   23 24 26 22

___ ___ ___ ___ ___ ___   ___ ___ ___ ___ ___
31 18 25 27 33 28   34 25 33 18 31

A=24	G=33	M=23	S=28	Y=39
B=36	H=18	N=27	T=31	Z=21
C=11	I=25	O=14	U=29	
D=19	J=30	P=37	V=35	
E=22	K=26	Q=13	W=17	
F=15	L=16	R=34	X=38	

Things to Do

- [ ] *If you do something wrong, say you're sorry right away.*
- [ ] *Ask a couple who has been married for a long time how they resolve conflict.*
- [ ] *Read Matthew 18:21-35. Think about which character you are most like and which you should be most like.*
- [ ] *Rewrite the story of Butch and Cassidy, showing how they worked out their conflict and how their lives would be different.*

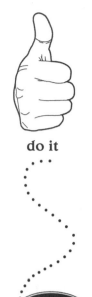

do it

Things to Remember

Pride leads to conflict; those who take advice are wise. – *Proverbs 13:10*

Even if that person wrongs you seven times a day and each time turns again and asks forgiveness, you must forgive. – *Luke 17:4*

If you are presenting a sacrifice at the altar in the Temple and you suddenly remember that someone has something against you, leave your sacrifice there at the altar. Go and be reconciled to that person. Then come and offer your sacrifice to God. – *Matthew 5:23-24*

Always be humble and gentle. Be patient with each other, making allowance for each other's faults because of your love. – *Ephesians 4:2*

If you forgive those who sin against you, your heavenly Father will forgive you. But if you refuse to forgive others, your Father will not forgive your sins. – *Matthew 6:14-15*

wisdom

Difficulties are meant to rouse, not discourage. The human spirit is to grow strong by conflict.

— *William Ellery Channing*

Man must evolve for all human conflict a method which rejects revenge, aggression and retaliation. The foundation of such a method is love.

— *Martin Luther King Jr.*

To err is human, to forgive divine.

— *Alexander Pope*

Stop Signs

A person with good
sense is respected;
a treacherous
person is headed
for destruction.
Proverbs 13:15

One of the fun attractions at an amusement park is the bumper cars. Bumper cars are fun because no matter how old you are, you can drive and bump into someone else. Jen can ram into Mom. Mom can crash into Grandpa, and Grandpa can bump little Jen. There are really no rules, so bumper cars can crash all they want.

While bumper cars are fun, you can't get very far that way. Can you imagine if people drove like bumper cars on the highway? The roads would be full of crashes everywhere. You couldn't drive to church, school, or the movies because every road would be covered in car pileups. This is why there are road signs and traffic lights, so people can drive safely and get where they need to go. People can be like cars to some degree. You may be like a bumper car, always trying to bump into things and have a good, fun time, but other people might not be like bumper cars. Some people are a little quieter and need their personal space from time to time.

Respecting other people is like respecting road signs. If your mom and dad need some quiet time, respect that and try to be quiet while they relax. Respecting people means trying to treat them how they like to be treated. In the Bible Paul says that you should "do all that you can to live in peace with everyone" (Romans 12:18). This means you shouldn't always try to get your way. If Jeff likes to play soccer instead of basketball, be respectful of his interests and play soccer with him sometimes. Or if Shellie doesn't like to talk, then don't try to make her talk.

You like it when you get to have your way, but so do other people. God made everyone a little different, and you should respect those differences. Even though you may like playing bumper cars, you might get tired of it if you were riding your bike when Jeff decided to drive his bumper car into your wheels.

Dear God, please help me to give up my way sometimes and to respect others' differences.

Crossword

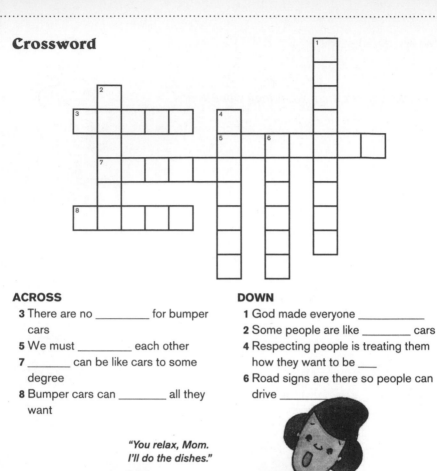

ACROSS

3 There are no _____ for bumper cars

5 We must _____ each other

7 _____ can be like cars to some degree

8 Bumper cars can _____ all they want

DOWN

1 God made everyone _____

2 Some people are like _____ cars

4 Respecting people is treating them how they want to be ___

6 Road signs are there so people can drive _____

"You relax, Mom. I'll do the dishes."

Things to Do

- ☐ *The next time you hang out with your friends, ask them what they want to do instead of doing what you want to do.*
- ☐ *Be respectful to people even when others are not.*
- ☐ *Read Romans 12, and write down ways Paul gives for living in harmony with others.*
- ☐ *Do the dishes for your parents this week so they can relax.*

do it

Things to Remember

wisdom

Make every effort to keep yourselves united in the Spirit, binding yourselves together with peace. *— Ephesians 4:3*

Love each other with genuine affection, and take delight in honoring each other.
— Romans 12:10

Sensible people control their temper; they earn respect by overlooking wrongs.
— Proverbs 19:11

Don't look out only for your own interests, but take an interest in others, too. *— Philippians 2:4*

Live in harmony with each other. Don't be too proud to enjoy the company of ordinary people. And don't think you know it all! *— Romans 12:16*

I'm not concerned with your liking or disliking me . . . All I ask is that you respect me as a human being.
— Jackie Robinson

Being brilliant is no great feat if you respect nothing.
— Johann Wolfgang von Goethe

Only those who respect the personality of others can be of real use to them.
— Albert Schweitzer

The Fire Swamp

Those who are peacemakers will plant seeds of peace and reap a harvest of righteousness.

James 3:18

In the movie *The Princess Bride*, the hero, Westley, and Buttercup get stuck in the Fire Swamp. This is a scary and dangerous place. One of the dangerous things in the Fire Swamp is a pit that is a bit like quicksand. If you step in it, you get stuck and start to sink. Buttercup gets stuck in this quicksand-like stuff, and Westley has to jump in to save her.

People get stuck in real life all the time. God has an answer for people when they get stuck. The Bible says that you reap what you sow. This means you get what you give. What most people do when they run into trouble is focus only on themselves. It's easy to worry only about your own troubles, but God asks his people to look at other people's needs and not just their own.

When you think of yourself and not other people, you often get stuck in your own Fire Swamp. The best thing to do is to help other people, because God says that when you do, you will be blessed. This doesn't mean you will get a bazillion dollars if you tithe from your allowance, but it might mean that the bike you've been wanting to get finally goes on sale and is cheap enough for you to pay for out of the money you've

saved up. Westley didn't worry about the Fire Swamp
or the Rodents Of Unusual Size surrounding him. He
saw that Buttercup needed help, and he jumped in
and rescued her. He got her unstuck by helping her
with her needs. If he had focused only on himself, he
might have gotten stuck, too.

When you help other people you actually
help yourself anyhow. Westley's reaction to save
Buttercup was a natural reaction because he loved
her. She was grateful to him for saving her, but had
he been selfish, he would have lost her forever. His
action of great love caused Buttercup to love him
even more. He reaped what he sowed.

pray

*Dear God,
please help me
to genuinely love
others and put
them first—to
sow love.*

"I heard you reap
what you sow."

Secret Codes

Cross out every C, D, F, G, J, K, M, N, Q, V, X, and Z to solve the secret code.

```
M K J F D C T Z Q X G Q H F V X J K E G F D C B M X M N Q V Z I J
K M B M K N V Z C D L D F G X J K M N E Z C D F K M Q V Z S N M
K J A C D F Q V Z Y K M N Q V S C D X G J K T N V Z X G H G A J X
G T D Y N M X J K Q V Z D C Q X J K O C U F G X K N V R Z V K J X
G E F D N M A F X J K Q V Z P F D W H A J K M N Q V T M K J Y C
O D F M N Q V Z U J K S F G D C O M X Z C D F G X J K V K M N W
```

___ ___ ___ ___

___ ___ ___ ___ ___ ___

___ ___ ___ ___ ___ ___

Use the key to solve the secret code.

A B C D E F G H I J K L M N O P Q R S T U V W X Y Z
≈ ′ ! @ # $ % ^ & * ( ) " Ï = + Ω ç √ ∫ Δ © ∂ β å π

___ ___ ___
! ≈ ç   # $ =   ç   ∫   ^   #

___ ___ ___ ___
Ï # # @ √   = $ = ∫ ^ # ç √

Thinking only of yourself can get you stuck.

176

Things to Do

do it

- ☐ *Ask your parents to tell you of a time when they reaped what they sowed.*
- ☐ *Donate some of your money to a charity that helps people in need.*
- ☐ *Ask your parents if you can plant some seeds in your backyard or in a kitchen herb garden. As the plants grow, think about what you can learn from this experience.*
- ☐ *Be careful at Morecambe Bay, England, because there's lots of quicksand there.*

Things to Remember

wisdom

The tongue can bring death or life; those who love to talk will reap the consequences. — *Proverbs 18:21*

So let's not get tired of doing what is good. At just the right time we will reap a harvest of blessing if we don't give up. — *Galatians 6:9*

Send your grain across the seas, and in time, profits will flow back to you. — *Ecclesiastes 11:1*

My experience shows that those who plant trouble and cultivate evil will harvest the same. — *Job 4:8*

Farmers who wait for perfect weather never plant. If they watch every cloud, they never harvest.

— *Ecclesiastes 11:4*

What we hope ever to do with ease, we must learn first to do with diligence.
— *Samuel Johnson*

Diligence is the mother of good fortune.
— *Benjamin Disraeli*

The leading rule for the lawyer, as for the man of every other calling, is diligence. Leave nothing for tomorrow which can be done today.
— *Abraham Lincoln*

Car Wash Sundays

read it

God's purpose in all this was to use the church to display his wisdom in its rich variety to all the unseen rulers and authorities in the heavenly places.

Ephesians 3:10

Cars are cool. Fast cars are very cool, and old fast cars are just plain awesome. Near Hollywood, California, is the oldest Big Boy restaurant in the country. On most Friday nights people from the area bring out their cool, old cars to show off to their friends and the tourists. Even famous people bring out their cars for everyone to see. There are Corvettes, Mustangs, and tons of other cars you might never have heard of. Each car looks like it is perfect. They're shiny and just about the best thing for a hundred miles.

But before those cars end up in the parking lot of the Big Boy, they are first washed and cleaned. In a big city like Hollywood, pollution and street gunk can get all over a car, so the owners make sure their cars are clean before showing them off.

People can get dirty too. In this world there are things that are not the best for you. Sin is like dirt and grime. You can get it on you just by being around it. Bad language at school or a fight that breaks out in your neighborhood can make an impact on you. This is why going to church is so important. Going to church is like going to a car wash every week. God likes it when his people set time aside every week to be with him. Doing something God likes is always a good thing, and going to church is especially good for you. By hanging out with other Christians and helping out at the church, you show God that he and his people are priorities in your life. You also allow yourself to encourage others and be encouraged. Church is a great place to start your week.

When people go to church, it's like getting those cars ready to show at Big Boy. No one is perfect—not even church people—but everyone should be a lot shinier and cleaner after they go. Going to church shows God that no matter what happens, you will make him a priority.

Dear God, thank you for my church family and for bringing us together each week.

"It's cool that something that makes me feel so good also pleases God."

Unscramble These Words

ins • hhccur • ypirtroi • sawdeh • alecden • meti •
gghnnai • stumsgan • rytid • cmipta • niehglp

Secret Code

21	6	18	13	14		14	3		9	5	10	12	2	15
+12	+8	+7	+14	+19		+17	+11		+2	+13	+19	+22	+9	+3

___ ___ ___ ___ ___   ___ ___   ___ ___ ___ ___ ___ ___

13	12	7	7	12		18	10	15	17		16	5	8
+15	+6	+7	+10	+16		+13	+8	+9	+14		+17	+9	+11

___ ___ ___ ___ ___   ___ ___ ___ ___   ___ ___ ___

13	12		11		16	11	12	9	25	11	13	28
+12	+16		+13		+21	+23	+13	+5	+9	+14	+18	+11

___ ___   ___   ___ ___ ___ ___ ___ ___ ___ ___

A=24	G=33	M=23	S=28	Y=39
B=36	H=18	N=27	T=31	Z=21
C=11	I=25	O=14	U=29	
D=19	J=30	P=37	V=35	
E=22	K=26	Q=13	W=17	
F=15	L=16	R=34	X=38	

"I don't need a bath! I got cleaned at church!"

Things to Do

- ☐ *If you haven't gone to church in a while, ask your parents if you can go.*
- ☐ *Pray and ask God to help you find a church to go to if you don't know where to go.*
- ☐ *This next week read Acts 2–4 to see how the early church got started.*
- ☐ *Write down ten reasons why you like going to church.*

do it
· · ·

Things to Remember

Let us not neglect our meeting together, as some people do, but encourage one another, especially now that the day of his return is drawing near. *– Hebrews 10:25*

I say to you that you are Peter (which means "rock"), and upon this rock I will build my church, and all the powers of hell will not conquer it. *– Matthew 16:18*

They worshiped together at the Temple each day, met in homes for the Lord's Supper, and shared their meals with great joy and generosity—all the while praising God and enjoying the goodwill of all the people. *– Acts 2:46-47*

Together, we are his house, built on the foundation of the apostles and the prophets. And the cornerstone is Christ Jesus himself. *– Ephesians 2:20*

And the church is his body; it is made full and complete by Christ, who fills all things everywhere with himself. *– Ephesians 1:23*

wisdom

Yes, I see the Church as the body of Christ. But, oh! How we have blemished and scarred that body through social neglect and through fear of being nonconformists.
– Martin Luther King Jr.

The difference between listening to a radio sermon and going to church . . . is almost like the difference between calling your girl on the phone and spending an evening with her.
– Dwight L. Moody

The Cowardly Lion

Jesus spoke to them at once. "Don't be afraid," he said. "Take courage. I am here!"

Matthew 14:27

In *The Wizard of Oz*, one of the main characters is the Cowardly Lion. Lions are supposed to be big and strong, but this one is weaker than a little kitten. His wish is to have courage. Eventually he gets his wish. In the Bible, one of Jesus' followers appears to be like the Cowardly Lion.

Peter was one of Jesus' most trusted followers. He walked on water with him for a short time, he saw Jesus feed thousands of people with only a few fish and some bread, and he saw Jesus raise people from the dead. However, when things got tough and Jesus was arrested, Peter denied that he had ever known Jesus. Peter got scared even when a small girl talked about his being a friend of Jesus.

Peter did not show courage during this time. Courage is doing what is right and taking a stand even when it might be tough to do so. When the superhero Flash rescues someone from a burning building, he shows he has courage because he, too, could get hurt if the building falls in from the flames. The same feat would not be so courageous for Superman, since there's nothing at stake for him.

Different situations require different types of courage. Having the type of courage that Flash has might be different from what you need. Having courage for you might mean you are not afraid to tell your friends at school about Jesus.

Peter had even told Jesus that he would never betray him, but he got scared and messed up. The good news is that Peter did grow in courage. In fact, God used Peter to lead his church after Jesus went to heaven. Peter even died for his faith in Jesus.

Even if you get scared at times, God can still use you and help you have more courage. Showing courage is kind of like working out: the more you do it, the easier it gets. You may not yet have the courage that Peter displayed, but over time you can be courageous if you keep trying.

pray

Dear God, please give me the courage to do what is right and the wisdom to know when to take a stand.

"I don't know when I was more afraid: telling James about Jesus or climbing that tree to get Mrs. Sampson's cat."

Secret Code

___ ___ ___   ___ ___ ___   ___ ___ ___ ___   ___ ___ ___   ___ ___ ___ ___
33 14 19   11 24 27   18 22 16 37   39 14 29   18 24 35 22

___ ___ ___ ___   ___ ___ ___ ___ ___ ___ ___
23 14 34 22   11 14 29 34 24 33 22

A=24 G=33 M=23 S=28 Y=39
B=36 H=18 N=27 T=31 Z=21
C=11 I=25 O=14 U=29
D=19 J=30 P=37 V=35
E=22 K=26 Q=13 W=17
F=15 L=16 R=34 X=38

"I would love to be a fire fighter—except I'm afraid of ladders."

Things to Do

- ☐ *Ask God to help you have more courage, and try sharing your faith in Jesus with a friend.*
- ☐ *Read about Peter in Matthew 26, John 21, and Acts 2. Write about the change that happened to Peter.*
- ☐ *Write down some of your favorite super-heroes and rate them from least courageous to most courageous.*
- ☐ *Ask your parents or other adults you trust about small ways you can increase your courage.*

do it

Things to Remember

This is my command—be strong and courageous! Do not be afraid or discouraged. For the LORD your God is with you wherever you go. *– Joshua 1:9*

Put on every piece of God's armor so you will be able to resist the enemy in the time of evil. Then after the battle you will still be standing firm. *– Ephesians 6:13*

But as for you, be strong and courageous, for your work will be rewarded. *– 2 Chronicles 15:7*

Wait patiently for the LORD. Be brave and courageous. Yes, wait patiently for the LORD. *– Psalm 27:14*

Be strong and courageous, all you who put your hope in the LORD! *– Psalm 31:24*

wisdom

If we're growing, we're always going to be out of our comfort zone.
— John Maxwell

Promise me you'll always remember: You're braver than you believe, and stronger than you seem, and smarter than you think.
— Christopher Robin in Winnie the Pooh

Courage is resistance to fear, mastery of fear—not absence of fear. *— Mark Twain*

The Cake Monster

A long time ago in the Land of Food, there lived an evil cake monster. The cake monster was big and bad and even had his own theme music, like Darth Vader. This villain's main goal was to rid the kingdom of every vegetable. The cake monster wanted to get all the kids to be his servants and work only for him. One day he found a group of kids eating a healthy meal, which made the cake monster angry. He knew if he could get them to eat junk food, they would be under his power. So he told them that if they would only eat some of his ice cream and fast food, then they would never have to eat anything healthy again. The kids pushed away their healthy meals, and the cake monster fed them as many pizzas, french fries, and jelly beans as they could eat. The cake monster laughed out loud because he knew he'd won. He commanded them to follow him, but they couldn't. They tried, but after eating so much junk food, none of them could move. The cake monster's plan failed big-time.

Eating sweets isn't always bad, but as the cake monster showed, eating *only* sweets isn't smart either. God wants his people to be healthy. First Corinthians says your body is a temple of the Holy Spirit, so you should keep your body healthy to give the Holy Spirit a good place to live. This doesn't mean it's wrong to have ice cream or pizza to celebrate a special occasion. But it *does* mean you shouldn't eat it all the time.

Another important way to stay healthy is exercising. Playing football, running, and riding your bike are all good ways to exercise. God made your body to get stronger the more you exercise, so stay active no matter what. If all you eat is junk, you aren't taking very good care of the Holy Spirit's temple. But if you eat right and exercise, your body has a better chance of staying healthy and doing a lot more for God.

pray

Dear God, thank you for allowing your Holy Spirit to live in me. Please help me keep his temple clean.

"It would be perfect if candy was good for you too."

Secret Code

```
  10    16    18    11    14    16        23    19    20     7    19          16    15
 +12    +8   +13   +14   +13   +17       +11    +6   +13   +11   +12          +9   +13
 ___   ___   ___   ___   ___   ___       ___   ___   ___   ___   ___         ___   ___


  13    12    21    21          21    11    26    15           5     7
 +17   +17    +7   +10         +16   +13    +8   +16          +9    +8
 ___   ___   ___   ___         ___   ___   ___   ___         ___   ___


  13    15    11    16    11    14    28         9    11     5     7     7     5    28
 +15   +16   +13   +23   +14   +13    +5        +9   +11   +19    +9   +24   +13   +11
 ___   ___   ___   ___   ___   ___   ___        ___  ___   ___   ___   ___   ___   ___
```

A=24   G=33   M=23   S=28   Y=39
B=36   H=18   N=27   T=31   Z=21
C=11   I=25   O=14   U=29
D=19   J=30   P=37   V=35
E=22   K=26   Q=13   W=17
F=15   L=16   R=34   X=38

"I like the exercise part of staying healthy a lot more than eating spinach."

188

Things to Do

- ☐ *The next time you think about eating cake, eat an apple instead.*
- ☐ *Try exercising every day this week for at least thirty minutes.*
- ☐ *Ask your teachers for some ideas on how to be healthy.*
- ☐ *Read 1 Corinthians 9:24-27. Then talk with your parents about how you as a family can eat better.*

do it

Things to Remember

wisdom

Refuse to worry, and keep your body healthy. — *Ecclesiastes 11:10*

Lord, your discipline is good, for it leads to life and health. You restore my health and allow me to live! — *Isaiah 38:16*

He makes the whole body fit together perfectly. As each part does its own special work, it helps the other parts grow, so that the whole body is healthy and growing and full of love. — *Ephesians 4:16*

Don't you realize that your body is the temple of the Holy Spirit, who lives in you and was given to you by God? You do not belong to yourself, for God bought you with a high price. So you must honor God with your body. — *1 Corinthians 6:19-20*

I discipline my body like an athlete, training it to do what it should. Otherwise, I fear that after preaching to others I myself might be disqualified. — *1 Corinthians 9:27*

Red meat is not bad for you. Now blue-green meat, that's bad for you! — *Tommy Smothers*

Eating properly is great. I mean you cut the fat down, cut the cholesterol out, but still you got to get your rest and you got to have some form of exercise. — *Mike Ditka*

The greatest wealth is health. — *Virgil*

The Game of Sorry

I confess my sins; I am deeply sorry for what I have done.

Psalm 38:18

Robbie's dad was gone a lot when he was growing up. His job made him travel all over the country. When Robbie's dad was home, he argued with Robbie's mom most of the time. Robbie loved his dad, but he didn't like hearing his parents fight. When his dad got angry, he said mean things to Robbie's mom and even to Robbie. After things calmed down, Robbie's dad felt bad about what he'd said, but he never said he was sorry. This hurt Robbie. As Robbie got older, he said mean things too, and like his dad, he never said he was sorry. Robbie really wanted to, but because he never saw his dad do it, he didn't know what to do.

Saying you're sorry can't change the bad things you've done, but it can show others that you know you did something wrong. Saying you're sorry helps other people heal and feel better. It also helps eliminate bitterness in relationships.

There is a board game named *Sorry!* In this game you are constantly making the other players start over again. When you bump another player, you say you're sorry. It isn't difficult since you don't really mean it. But saying you're sorry in life is really important— and sometimes hard to do. Even if you know people who never say they're sorry, that doesn't mean you shouldn't apologize when you make mistakes. You honor God when you tell him you're sorry after you make a mistake, and you honor him when you apologize to others, too. In fact, God is more likely to hear your prayers when you say you're sorry to your friends and family than when you don't (see Matthew 5:23-26). So if you get in a fight with Jeff at school or get angry with your dad at home, it's important that you say you're sorry. Saying you're sorry to God is like pushing a restart button. God is eager to forgive sin because of what Jesus did for us. But you can't start over if you don't first admit that you've made a mistake.

pray

Dear God, I'm sorry for my sins. Please help me to acknowledge when I'm wrong and to apologize when I hurt others.

Saying you're sorry might not change what you did, but it helps to admit you were wrong.

Crossword

ACROSS

5 You honor God when you _____ to others

8 You should apologize when you make _____

9 You can't start over if you don't _____ you've made a mistake

DOWN

1 Saying you're sorry can't _____ the bad things you've done

2 Saying you're sorry can show others that you _____ you did something wrong

3 You _____ God when you tell him you are sorry

4 Saying you're sorry _____ other people feel better

6 Saying you're sorry is _____ in life

7 Saying you're sorry is like pushing a _____ button

Saying you're sorry gives the other person a chance to forgive you.

Things to Do

- [ ] *Say you're sorry as soon as you realize you've made a mistake.*
- [ ] *Play the board game* Sorry! *with your family this week.*
- [ ] *Ask your parents to tell you of a time when apologizing helped them.*
- [ ] *Write a poem about the importance of saying you're sorry.*

do it

Things to Remember

The kind of sorrow God wants us to experience leads us away from sin and results in salvation. There's no regret for that kind of sorrow. But worldly sorrow, which lacks repentance, results in spiritual death.
— 2 Corinthians 7:10

wisdom

"Don't sin by letting anger control you." Don't let the sun go down while you are still angry, for anger gives a foothold to the devil.
— Ephesians 4:26-27

If you are presenting a sacrifice at the altar in the Temple and you suddenly remember that someone has something against you, leave your sacrifice there at the altar. Go and be reconciled to that person. Then come and offer your sacrifice to God. *— Matthew 5:23-24*

When he told us how much you long to see me, and how sorry you are for what happened, and how loyal you are to me, I was filled with joy! *— 2 Corinthians 7:7*

Fools make fun of guilt, but the godly acknowledge it and seek reconciliation. *— Proverbs 14:9*

Love in the real world means saying you're sorry 10 times a day.
— Kathie Lee Gifford

Never ruin an apology with an excuse.
— Kimberly Johnson

Love is always having to say I'm sorry. *— Bob Irwin*

Waterfalls and Diapers

read it

Ever since the world was created, people have seen the earth and sky. Through everything God made, they can clearly see his invisible qualities.
Romans 1:20

Austin was like most boys his age. He played baseball and rode his bike. But unlike most kids his age, he didn't have any parents. He was an orphan. He didn't know where his parents were, but somehow he did believe in God. One night when he was feeling lonely, he looked out his window and asked God if he could hear him. He asked if God could let him know he wasn't alone. Just moments after he prayed, he saw a shooting star. And then after the first star came many more. It was like a fireworks show in the night sky. Austin knew it was more than a show, though. He knew it was God talking back to him. Austin was not alone, because God was looking out for him.

God is an amazing God. When you look at nature, you can see a lot of his personal character. You can see his strength in the big mountains. You can see his beauty in a bunch of flowers. You can see his friendliness in a playful dog. God created so many amazing things for you to enjoy. Nature is one sign of his great love for you. For example, you need water to drink, so he could have just made water appear in a regular hole in the ground only, but he also gave you waterfalls and rivers. When God makes things, he does it right. All of the truly awesome things in the world are God inspired. God could have made everything boring or gross like baby diapers or ugly concrete, but he didn't. God created asteroids and waves to surf and dirt to dig up!

God can even speak to you through nature like he did with Austin. This doesn't mean that your Christmas tree will start talking to you next year (unless you have a Douglas Fir Singing Tree), but it does mean that when you look at nature it reveals a part of God that you can see if you take the time.

Dear God, thank you for showing me who you are through nature. Please show me how to take care of your world.

"How could anyone see this and not know there is a God?"

Secret Codes

Cross out every B, C, F, J, L, P, Q, U, V, X, Y, and Z to solve the secret code.

L P Q U V W B J F L H C V X Y E L P J F N B B F L P B C F G J F O U D
Z Y B C F L P M B F J L C A V U Q P L K F C B Y Z E P L J S C B F J S O
J L P Q M B C F E U V Z Y T L P F C B H L J F I Q U V X Y N J B C F G Q
H Y X V U E L J F C D B C O U V Z Y L J E F C B L P S Q U V Z Y Z I B
C F J L P T L J F C B R Q U V L J F V X I V Q G L J C B H P Q L J F C B T

__ __ __ __ __   __ __ __ __   __ __ __ __ __ __

__ __ __ __ __ __ __ __ __ __ __   __ __ __   __ __ __ __ __

__ __   __ __ __ __ __ __

Use the key to solve the secret code.

A B C D E F G H I J K L M N O P Q R S T U V W X Y Z
≈ ´ ! @ # $ % ^ & * ( ) " Ï = + Ω ç √ ∫ Δ © ∂ ß å π

__ __ __ __ __ __ __ __ __ __ __ __
% = @ ! ç # ≈ ∫ # @ √ =

__ __ __ __ __ __ __ __ __ __ __
" ≈ Ï å ≈ " ≈ π & Ï %

__ __ __ __ __ __ __ __ __ __ __ __
∫ ^ & Ï % √ $ = ç å = Δ

__ __ __ __ __ __ __
∫ = # Ï * = å

"Rover didn't enjoy the nature hike, but I sure did!"

Things to Do

- ☐ *Go on a picnic with your family to a park and enjoy the grass and trees.*
- ☐ *Thank God for things in nature that you like when you see them or think about them.*
- ☐ *Ask your parents how they most like to enjoy nature.*
- ☐ *Find a book on zoology and look through the pictures. Make a list of your favorites, and thank God for his diverse world.*

do it

Things to Remember

The mountains quaked in the presence of the LORD, the God of Mount Sinai—in the presence of the LORD, the God of Israel.
– Judges 5:5

Even the sparrow finds a home, and the swallow builds her nest and raises her young at a place near your altar, O LORD of Heaven's Armies, my King and my God!
– Psalm 84:3

The heavens proclaim the glory of God. The skies display his craftsmanship. *– Psalm 19:1*

You will live in joy and peace. The mountains and hills will burst into song, and the trees of the field will clap their hands! *– Isaiah 55:12*

You are dressed in a robe of light. You stretch out the starry curtain of the heavens; you lay out the rafters of your home in the rain clouds. You make the clouds your chariot; you ride upon the wings of the wind.
– Psalm 104:2-3

wisdom

In all things of nature there is something of the marvelous.
– Aristotle

The least movement is of importance to all nature. The entire ocean is affected by a pebble.
– Blaise Pascal

For in the true nature of things, if we rightly consider, every green tree is far more glorious than if it were made of gold and silver.
– Martin Luther

No Laughing Matter

Matt liked to joke about Jon because Jon was big for his age. Matt would make up jokes about Jon being King Kong and Godzilla. A lot of the kids at school laughed at his jokes, so Matt felt good about himself. Jon, however, felt like mud. Jon knew he was big for his age and often cried when everyone else made fun of him. What Jon didn't know is that Matt only joked about his size because he was insecure about his own size. Matt was short for his age, so he figured instead of kids making fun of him, he would get them making fun of Jon.

Humor, like a basketball court, has boundaries. When you go out of bounds, you lose the ball, and if you do that too much, you lose the game. There are a few different ways to use humor the wrong way. When you tell jokes about other people that make them feel bad, that's wrong. Making fun of someone else isn't funny; it's just mean. Another form of bad humor is telling jokes about things you shouldn't be talking about. Kids at school may say things you know are wrong, but that doesn't mean you should. These types of jokes can sometimes use cusswords or talk about girls in a bad way. These types of jokes are told when guys try to act older and tougher than they are. A real man doesn't need to tell bad jokes to feel big and tough. A guy who doesn't have to tell bad jokes to make himself feel good is more of a man than one who makes fun of others or uses words he knows he shouldn't use.

God created humor, just like he created the moon and sun, so if you tell jokes and like to be funny, do it in a way that makes God proud. When you tell good jokes, God laughs at them too. He enjoys humor, so be sure to do it the right way.

pray

Dear God, please help me to know the boundaries of jokes. Help me use humor to build up rather than tear down.

What's funny to one can be hurtful to another.

Unscramble These Words

rumho • urpod • kjseo • earisnobud • saktlelabb • amne •
hutoegr • rsuicene • drloe

Secret Codes

10		16	9	11	14		6	16	19		6	3	10	16
+14		+18	+13	+13	+2		+17	+8	+8		+13	+11	+12	+12

13	6	21		21	6	11	11		15	5		8	14	11	7
+14	+8	+10		+6	+16	+11	+8		+16	+9		+23	+8	+5	+9

13	8	11		16	5	13	17	23
+23	+16	+8		+14	+9	+13	+5	+5

A=24   G=33   M=23   S=28   Y=39
B=36   H=18   N=27   T=31   Z=21
C=11   I=25   O=14   U=29
D=19   J=30   P=37   V=35
E=22   K=26   Q=13   W=17
F=15   L=16   R=34   X=38

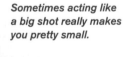

*Sometimes acting like
a big shot really makes
you pretty small.*

Things to Do

- [ ] *Write down at least three jokes from a joke book or from your memory.*
- [ ] *Ask your parents to tell you their favorite jokes ever. Then tell them the jokes you wrote down.*
- [ ] *With your parents' permission, watch a moviy, likee that is very funn Elf. Then journal about which jokes are okay and which jokes are not God-pleasing.*
- [ ] *If you have pushed a joke too far with one of your friends or classmates, apologize to him or her.*

do it

wisdom

Things to Remember

Obscene stories, foolish talk, and coarse jokes—these are not for you. Instead, let there be thankfulness to God. — *Ephesians 5:4*

May the LORD smile on you and be gracious to you. — *Numbers 6:25*

They sharpen their tongues like swords and aim their bitter words like arrows. — *Psalm 64:3*

Just as damaging as a madman shooting a deadly weapon is someone who lies to a friend and then says, "I was only joking." — *Proverbs 26:18-19*

Watch your tongue and keep your mouth shut, and you will stay out of trouble. — *Proverbs 21:23*

Through humor, you can soften some of the worst blows that life delivers. And once you find laughter, no matter how painful your situation might be, you can survive it. — *Bill Cosby*

The kind of humor I like is the thing that makes me laugh for five seconds and think for ten minutes. — *William Davis*

Humor is a rubber sword—it allows you to make a point without drawing blood. — *Mary Hirsch*

Roller Coasters, Hockey, and Learning How to Lose

Above all, you must live as citizens of heaven, conducting yourselves in a manner worthy of the Good News about Christ.
Philippians 1:27

Nick was a good hockey player. He was the best goalie in his league. His team was the favorite to win the championship this year, but things did not go as his coaches had planned. Nick gave up three goals, and his team, the Flint Wolverines, lost the game 3-2. After the game Nick hung his head in shame and expected his parents to be angry or really sad, but they weren't mad or sad. Instead of crying their eyes out or yelling their heads off, Nick's parents took him to Cedar Point, the best roller coaster park in the world. Nick had a blast, but he wondered why he got rewarded for losing. He asked his dad why they were celebrating instead of bawling their eyes out about the game. His dad told him that winning isn't everything. He also said, "When you give your best and work your hardest, you do win. You can't always control if you win or lose, but you can choose to be a good loser." His dad also pointed out that it is okay to want to win, but when a game is over, you can't change that you lost, so it's best to celebrate the effort. Nick asked if he would get to go to Cedar Point every time he lost. His dad responded, "No, but we brought you to the park because you worked hard and never ever gave up. So you didn't lose in our eyes. You got this reward for winning—winning our respect."

First Corinthians 10:31 points out that everything you do should be for the glory of God. This is true even when you lose. You can honor God by being a good loser. This doesn't mean that you will *like* to lose, but that you will lose with grace and celebrate the victories you did have. No one likes a sore loser, but everyone respects a good loser—even God. When you play something, give it your best, but if you don't win, be your best by being a good loser.

pray

Dear God, please help me to give my best in everything and to accept defeat with grace when I lose.

Celebrating is OK. Celebrating like a gorilla hyped up on candy is not.

Word Search

REWARD   CELEBRATE   BEST   HONOR   CONTROL   EFFORT
SHAME   ANGRY   LOSER   WORKED   GRACE

D	B	D	K	W	O	R	K	E	D	P	T	U	E	J	L	M
S	U	T	G	E	S	G	P	C	D	B	B	Y	C	U	T	Y
H	V	N	O	I	E	W	I	U	E	O	E	L	K	R	V	H
A	O	P	T	R	T	G	H	J	O	D	S	B	N	R	N	N
M	T	R	F	C	E	L	E	B	R	A	T	E	I	R	R	D
E	U	W	E	W	S	W	W	D	U	X	F	V	D	E	D	G
V	G	V	W	Y	N	R	A	L	G	F	E	D	L	S	O	R
B	J	T	T	P	H	N	D	R	O	T	D	U	O	O	Y	A
V	J	R	P	L	G	T	G	H	D	R	V	L	R	L	W	C
R	O	O	I	R	L	E	K	J	T	U	T	B	B	M	R	E
W	G	F	Y	B	O	F	J	R	Y	G	U	N	F	D	Y	N
V	M	F	O	U	R	C	R	O	N	O	H	P	O	O	R	P
W	S	E	A	D	F	K	N	J	H	G	Y	T	U	C	W	D
K	F	J	G	U	T	F	D	G	J	F	H	G	G	T	T	E

Secret Code

___ ___ ___ ___ ___ ___ ___ ___   ___ ___ ___ ___ ___ ___ ___ ___ ___
22 35 22 34 39 14 27 22   34 22 28 37 22 11 31 28   24

___ ___ ___ ___   ___ ___ ___ ___ ___
33 14 14 19   16 14 28 22 34

A=24   G=33   M=23   S=28   Y=39
B=36   H=18   N=27   T=31   Z=21
C=11   I=25   O=14   U=29
D=19   J=30   P=37   V=35
E=22   K=26   Q=13   W=17
F=15   L=16   R=34   X=38

Things to Do

- ☐ *If you get beat in something, celebrate your hard work and tell the winner how well they did.*
- ☐ *Ask your dad who he thinks is the classiest athlete in sports and why.*
- ☐ *Ask for permission to watch the movie* Rudy *and write down how the main character responded to losing.*
- ☐ *After getting permission, Google Joe Dumars and the Bad Boys. Research how Dumars was a good sport against Michael Jordan and the Chicago Bulls even when his teammates weren't.*

do it

Things to Remember

wisdom

What do you benefit if you gain the whole world but lose your own soul? Is anything worth more than your soul? *— Matthew 16:26*

Watch out that you do not lose what we have worked so hard to achieve. Be diligent so that you receive your full reward. *— 2 John 1:8*

Therefore, since God in his mercy has given us this new way, we never give up. *— 2 Corinthians 4:1*

That is why we never give up. Though our bodies are dying, our spirits are being renewed every day. *— 2 Corinthians 4:16*

Let's not get tired of doing what is good. At just the right time we will reap a harvest of blessing if we don't give up. *— Galatians 6:9*

Win as if you were used to it, lose as if you enjoyed it for a change.
— Ralph Waldo Emerson

When you win, say nothing. When you lose, say less.
— Paul Brown

The greatest test of courage on earth is to bear defeat without losing heart.
— Robert Ingersoll

Balloon Heads

read it

Pride goes before destruction, and haughtiness before a fall.

Proverbs 16:18

I n 2004 the NBA championship game had the Los Angeles Lakers against the Detroit Pistons. The Lakers were the heavy favorites, and everyone expected them to win in four easy games. The Lakers had a bunch of stars like Shaquille O'Neal and Kobe Bryant, but the Pistons had a group of hardworking guys. The Lakers thought they could simply walk into the game and be handed the trophy. They were overconfident. The Detroit Pistons won the championship in five games. A group of mostly noname players beat the Lakers like David beat Goliath.

It's easy for people to get overconfident. They are like balloon heads. When someone gets prideful and overconfident, their head grows like a balloon. What they don't realize is that the larger their heads get, the easier it is to pop their balloon. The Bible says that pride comes before a fall and that "God opposes the proud but favors the humble" (1 Peter 5:5). This means that when people think too much of themselves, God will soon change that. Sometimes when people win, they gloat and talk big, but God doesn't like that at all. This is one of the reasons he was with David when David beat Goliath.

Winning is not bad. In fact, winning is good because it shows how hard you've worked. But it's important to win with class. Bragging, talking trash, and taunting other people is not being a good winner. An example of being a good winner is the great running back Barry Sanders. When he scored a touchdown, he didn't spike it or dance. All he did was hand the ball to the referee. Sanders is one of the best NFL players of all time, and he is known as one of the classiest players ever too.

God wants you to be a good winner. Show respect to those you play against because you won't always win. Sometimes you will lose, and you won't enjoy it if the other guys are mean or rude. Set the example and don't be a balloon head.

pray

Dear God, even though I like to win, please help me not to be a balloon head, but to be a good winner.

SPELLING BEE

"Can you believe it? Three in a row! I get better every year."

Secret Codes

Add these numbers to solve the secret code.

10	6	14	18		14	6		16
+9	+8	+13	+13		+22	+16		+8

—— —— —— ——   —— ——   ——

22	16	10	9	6	11	11		9	15	5	14
+14	+8	+6	+7	+8	+3	+16		+9	+7	+19	+5

—— —— —— —— —— —— ——   —— —— —— ——

A=24	G=33	M=23	S=28	Y=39
B=36	H=18	N=27	T=31	Z=21
C=11	I=25	O=14	U=29	
D=19	J=30	P=37	V=35	
E=22	K=26	Q=13	W=17	
F=15	L=16	R=34	X=38	

Cross out the number of letters indicated and use the next letter to solve the secret code.

—— ——   —— ——   —— —— —— —— —— —— —— ——

—— ——   —— —— ——   —— —— —— ——

—— —— ——   —— —— ——

3, 2, 5, 3, 4, 6, 5, 2, 3, 4, 1, 5, 3, 5, 8, 7, 2, 6, 4, 5, 1, 5, 7, 3, 5, 4, 7

IMHILHTGTEDWIOKYSHEDTIPKIUTRMJTGREPJR
OOMGRTEDCTPAJYTFRNOJRTORMDWTOUYTRF
EWOYRFCNHKWPYITGEDTBNNGDEWIJYRDILTFE
WSCHPITGBCDCOYVLKJFREATRDVSUFERSCVS

Things to Do

- [ ] *Instead of talking trash, compliment other players.*
- [ ] *Ask your grandpa to name the best athlete he ever cheered for when he was a kid. Research this athlete to find out more about him or her.*
- [ ] *Draw a picture of how good you feel when you win.*
- [ ] *Write 1 Peter 5:5 on an index card and put it in a place where you'll see it often to remind yourself to be a good winner.*

do it

Things to Remember

Haughtiness goes before destruction; humility precedes honor. — *Proverbs 18:12*

The LORD detests the proud; they will surely be punished. — *Proverbs 16:5*

God blesses those who are humble, for they will inherit the whole earth. — *Matthew 5:5*

I will not tolerate people who slander their neighbors. I will not endure conceit and pride. — *Psalm 101:5*

But he gives us even more grace to stand against such evil desires. As the Scriptures say, "God opposes the proud but favors the humble." — *James 4:6*

wisdom

A winner is someone who recognizes his God-given talents, works his tail off to develop them into skills, and uses these skills to accomplish his goals. — *Larry Bird*

When the upper hand is ours, may we have the ability to handle the win with the dignity that we absorbed the loss. — *Doug Williams*

The Buying Flu

Work willingly at whatever you do, as though you were working for the Lord rather than for people.
Colossians 3:23

The grasshopper liked to spend everything he had. He liked toys and games and everything that was fun. The ant liked all those things too, but he saved his money for later in case he needed it. The grasshopper never saved his money and often laughed at the ant for being so boring. But one day the grasshopper stopped laughing. Winter came, and it was tough. The grasshopper ran out of food and money. The ant had lots of food stored up and lots of money if needed. The grasshopper asked the ant for help, and even though the grasshopper had been mean to him, the ant helped him anyway.

It is never too early to start saving money. When you get an allowance or mow a lawn, you should save like the ant did. When you get money, the first thing you should do is tithe 10 percent of it. Tithing is giving back to God what is his by giving to your local church. So if you make ten bucks, you should give one dollar to the church. After you tithe, the next thing you should do is save another 10 percent. If your parents have a bank account for you, put it in there. Otherwise get a piggy bank or small safe. So if you make ten dollars, one dollar goes to God and another dollar gets saved for a rainy day. This gives you eight dollars to spend.

Many people today spend money like they have a buying flu. They buy and buy to help them feel better, but God wants you to be wise with your money. In Ephesians 4:28 the Bible says that part of why we make money is to use that money to help others. Since God is the one who helps you get money, it is really his; he puts you in charge of it, and it is your job to use your money wisely. The ant not only saved his money, but he saved the grasshopper, too. Try to be an ant, not a grasshopper.

pray

Dear God, please help me to know how you would like me to use my money.

"I know this makes God happy, but I didn't know it would make me feel good too."

Crossword

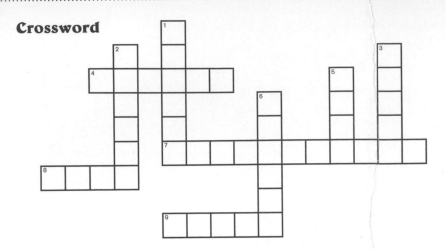

ACROSS

4 Tithing is giving to God by giving to your local _____

7 Try to be an ant and not a _____

8 It's never too early to _____ money

9 God is the one who helps you get

_____

DOWN

1 The grasshopper often laughed at the ant for being so _____

2 God has put you in _____ of the money you get

3 You should always give a _____ to your local church

5 The Bible says we make money in order to _____ others

6 You need to use money _____

"Why save? I don't think any rainy days are coming."

Things to Do

- Get a piggy bank, small safe, or bank account, and start saving 10 percent of what you earn. You might also save any change you get, like quarters and nickels.
- Ask your parents for some tips on how to save your money.
- Collect pop cans and mow lawns to make some extra money to save.
- Choose a charity to donate money to, and talk to your friends about helping to save for the donation.

do it

Things to Remember

Take a lesson from the ants, you lazybones. Learn from their ways and become wise! – *Proverbs 6:6*

A house is built by wisdom and becomes strong through good sense. Through knowledge its rooms are filled with all sorts of precious riches and valuables.
– *Proverbs 24:3-4*

wisdom

A penny saved is a penny earned.
– *Benjamin Franklin*

Make all you can, save all you can, give all you can.
– *John Wesley*

On the first day of each week, you should each put aside a portion of the money you have earned. Don't wait until I get there and then try to collect it all at once. – *1 Corinthians 16:2*

Good planning and hard work lead to prosperity, but hasty shortcuts lead to poverty. – *Proverbs 21:5*

The safest way to double your money is to fold it over once and put it in your pocket.
– *Kin Hubbard*

The wise have wealth and luxury, but fools spend whatever they get. – *Proverbs 21:20*

The North Star of Life

Jack and Kate got lost in the woods. They didn't know where to go. They didn't know which way was north or south. Jack remembered that their campsite was on the north side of the island, so if he could figure out which way was north, they would be okay. Then he looked up in the sky and saw the North Star. This let him know which way was north, so he and Kate ran north and finally found their campsite.

Sometimes you may feel lost and might not know what to do, but Jesus is like the North Star. Jesus can always show you the right path to take, because when you look to his example, he shows you the right things to do. Jesus set an example for you of what to do and what not to do. When you get into an argument with a friend, Jesus wants you to ask for forgiveness as soon as possible. He also says not to worry so much about little things but to focus on him.

Jesus is the ultimate compass in life. His way is always best. If you play baseball, you'd love to get advice from Albert Pujols. If you play football, how cool would it be to get Tom Brady to coach you on how to throw the ball? Similarly, Jesus is the champion of life. He lived a sinless life that was pleasing to God, and you have him to show you how to live. Throughout the New Testament you can read about the great things that Jesus did, so take a look. There are a lot of role models out there that you could look up to, but only one of them will never let you down and only one of them has ever died for you.

If Jack and Kate hadn't looked north, they would still be lost. Don't forget to look to your North Star, Jesus, because he can help get you on the right path if you let him.

Dear God, thank you for sending Jesus as an example to follow. Please help me to be more like Jesus.

"It's easy to ask, 'What Would Jesus Do?' It's harder to listen to the answer."

Secret Code

Cross out every B, D, F, K, M, Q, V, X, and Z to solve the secret code.

K M B F D J Q V X Z B D E K K M S B V X M K Z U B X Z Q V M Z S
B D V K M Q V C F M A M B D B N X Z Q D F A B D F F K M L Q V D
F X W Z B D K M Q V A F D B Y Q V X Z S Q K M B D S K F B X Z H
Z O M K X F D B W V X Z Y B D V K M O M K Q B D U V X Z T F D K
M H D B K M E K M Q V R D I K B X Q Z F D K G B D K B M H Q V M
K T D F X B P Z X V A Q M K Z F T B D V K M Q V X Z D B F K M H

—— —— —— —— ——   —— —— —— ——   —— —— —— —— —— ——

—— —— —— —— ——   —— —— —— ——   —— —— ——

—— —— —— —— ——   —— —— —— ——

Knowing who to listen to is a big part of doing what Jesus wants.

Things to Do

- ☐ *Read the book of Matthew over the next month. Write down your impressions of Jesus and try to be like him.*
- ☐ *Ask your pastor what his favorite attribute of Jesus is and how he tries to follow in Jesus' steps.*
- ☐ *Write a skit about what it would be like if you were more like Jesus.*
- ☐ *When you aren't sure what to do, try to think how Jesus would act in that situation and do as he would do.*

do it

Things to Remember

wisdom

And now, just as you accepted Christ Jesus as your Lord, you must continue to follow him. — *Colossians 2:6*

Those who say they live in God should live their lives as Jesus did. — *1 John 2:6*

Jesus . . . said, "I am the light of the world. If you follow me, you won't have to walk in darkness, because you will have the light that leads to life." — *John 8:12*

Then he said to the crowd, "If any of you wants to be my follower, you must turn from your selfish ways, take up your cross daily, and follow me." — *Luke 9:23*

Then Jesus said, "Come to me, all of you who are weary and carry heavy burdens, and I will give you rest. Take my yoke upon you. Let me teach you, because I am humble and gentle at heart, and you will find rest for your souls." — *Matthew 11:28-29*

Jesus Christ: The meeting place of eternity and time, the blending of deity and humanity, the junction of heaven and earth. — *Anonymous*

You cannot go outside of A and Z in the realm of literature; likewise Christ Jesus is First and Last of God's new creation, and all that is in between; you cannot get outside of that. — *T. Austin Sparks*

Scrooge Gets Robbed

read it

And I am praying that you will put into action the generosity that comes from your faith as you understand and experience all the good things we have in Christ.

Philemon 1:6

The story of Scrooge is one of the most famous Christmas stories of all time. Ebenezer Scrooge cares only about money and is a mean old man who treats his family and workers like dirt. During the story he sees his past, present, and future and finally decides that he wants to live a different life. He realizes that if he keeps on living as he has been, he will be miserable forever. His money couldn't save him no matter how much he had.

But what would have happened if Scrooge got robbed before he learned his lesson? He would have ended up poor and grumpy. He's lucky he didn't wait too long. Stuff doesn't last forever. Money doesn't last. Video games get old. Comic books get ripped and torn. Everything you have gets old. Scrooge learned the importance of giving, but many people today have not learned the same lesson. Seeing actors and sports players doing some of the dumb stuff they do, it's clear they need to learn what Scrooge learned.

God wants you to be generous. Generosity is being willing to give what you have to those who have less than you do. Being generous also means giving more than you really need to. Scrooge bought a poor family a turkey, but he didn't buy just any old turkey—he bought the best one in the store. For you, being generous might mean giving not an old basketball jersey to someone this year, but rather one of your newer ones that you really like and still use.

Being young, you might not have much money, but you can be generous with your time. Offer to hang out with people you wouldn't normally hang with. Scrooge went over to see a guy who worked for him. Sometimes being generous means helping someone who isn't your favorite person. Perhaps the annoying kid wants you to throw the football with him or your younger siblings want you to play dress-up. Scrooge learned the value of generosity. Make sure you do too.

pray

Dear God, please help me not to hold tightly to what is mine but to give generously to others.

"I don't even play this game anymore, but I bet somebody else would like it."

Word Search

GENEROUS GIVE POOR WILLING ROBBED
LEARNED GRUMPY LESS FAVORITE ANNOYING
FOOTBALL JERSEY SCROOGE

```
D B D K U T L E A R N E D E J L M
S U T G E S G P C D B F Y C U T Y
G V N E I E W I U E O S L K R V H
I O P N E T P H G N I L L I W N I
Y T R E T B O O K L J H D I P R D
Y U W R I S J W O U X F V D N D S
E G V O R N R U N R F E D L F O R
S R G U O D F G I V E D U O O Y E
R U U S V E E G H F X V L R U W Y
E M P I A L E B J T U S S E L R P
J P F Q F O F J B Y G U I F D Y N
V Y F O U R C B F O O T B A L L P
S C R O O G E N J H R Y T U R W D
K F J G U T F D G N I Y O N N A E
```

"Don't worry if you don't have money. I just got my allowance. I'll pay."

Things to Do

- ☐ *Pick out a game, jersey, or comic and ask your parents if it's okay to donate it to charity.*
- ☐ *If you have money, offer to buy someone a snack at the baseball game who might not be able to afford soda or nachos.*
- ☐ *Ask someone who doesn't have many friends to hang out sometime.*
- ☐ *Let your brother or sister play your video game or use your stuff first for a change.*

do it

Things to Remember

wisdom

Generous people plan to do what is generous, and they stand firm in their generosity. — *Isaiah 32:8*

They worshiped together at the Temple each day, met in homes for the Lord's Supper, and shared their meals with great joy and generosity. — *Acts 2:46*

They are being tested by many troubles, and they are very poor. But they are also filled with abundant joy, which has overflowed in rich generosity. — *2 Corinthians 8:2*

God is the one who provides seed for the farmer and then bread to eat. In the same way, he will provide and increase your resources and then produce a great harvest of generosity in you. — *2 Corinthians 9:10*

As a result of your ministry, they will give glory to God. For your generosity to them and to all believers will prove that you are obedient to the Good News of Christ. — *2 Corinthians 9:13*

Do all the good you can, by all the means you can, in all the ways you can, in all the places you can, at all the times you can, to all the people you can, as long as ever you can.
— *John Wesley*

If you can't feed a hundred people, then feed just one.
— *Mother Teresa*

We make a living by what we get, but we make a life by what we give.
— *Winston Churchill*

Truth or Dare

May integrity and honesty protect me, for I put my hope in you.

Psalm 25:21

I n Disney's *Pinocchio*, the nose of the puppet grows every time he tells a lie. Could you imagine if your nose grew when you lied? What if your ears got bigger or your head got larger or your lips turned purple when you lied? How would you look? You would look like some funny cartoon character if you didn't tell the truth. On the bright side, you'd probably tell the truth more often, because no one would want their head to grow to the size of the moon!

Pinocchio ends up learning to tell the truth, but not until he runs into a ton of trouble that almost gets him killed. You see, when you lie, you hurt not only yourself, but also those around you. Eventually lies come out, and when they do, it will be harder for your parents, teachers, and friends to trust you. One of the Ten Commandments is, "Do not lie or your ears will grow to the size of a truck!" Okay, it doesn't say anything about a truck, but the Bible says over and over again that you shouldn't lie because God is a God of truth. It reflects poorly on him when we lie.

Here are some important tips. First, don't lie. Second, if you have told a lie, the best thing to do is go to the person you lied to and tell them the truth.

It's better that they find out from you than from someone else. Third, remember that you can't keep up with all the lies. Sooner or later you'll slip up and the truth will get out. Fourth, if friends try to get you to lie, they are not real friends. Finally and most importantly, don't lie.

Some people lie to get out of trouble, but usually lying only gets you into more trouble. You want to be the kid that everyone can trust, so don't give them any reason to doubt you. It's better to own up to doing something wrong now than to lie, making it worse later.

pray

Dear God, please help me not to lie. Help me to have the courage to tell the truth even when it hurts.

"Really, Dad, Zippy did it!"

Secret Codes

Add these numbers to solve the secret code.

7	27	12	14	11		6	16	5	25		14	18	9	12
+9	+12	+13	+13	+22		+8	+11	+11	+14		+19	+4	+22	+16
___	___	___	___	___		___	___	___	___		___	___	___	___

26	3	10		12	16		11	11	9	15
+13	+11	+19		+13	+11		+12	+3	+25	+7
___	___	___		___	___		___	___	___	___

22	16	10	18	16	11	11
+9	+18	+4	+11	+20	+5	+11
___	___	___	___	___	___	___

A=24	E=22	I=25	M=23	Q=13	U=29	Y=39
B=36	F=15	J=30	N=27	R=34	V=35	Z=21
C=11	G=33	K=26	O=14	S=28	W=17	
D=19	H=18	L=16	P=37	T=31	X=38	

Cross out the number of letters indicated and use the next letter to solve the secret code.

___ ___ ___ ___ ___ ___ ___ ___ ___ ___ ___ ___ ___

___ ___ ___ ___ ___ ___ ___ ___ ___ ___ ___ ___ ___ ___

___ ___ ___ ___ ___ ___ ___ ___ ___ ___ ___ ___ ___ ___ ___

3, 2, 5, 3, 4, 6, 5, 2, 3, 4, 1, 5, 3, 5, 8, 7, 2, 6, 4, 5, 1, 5, 7, 3, 5, 4, 7,
6, 4, 2, 7, 1, 5, 6, 3, 2, 5, 4

O J H I M N T K J H Y T I F G T S F R E W H I K M N B G A G T O L M
R D S D Y T E F C D R Y O J R P H Y R D P J N G E I K H Y T O B G T
R E D C S P P O K M N G R L T B E O K M N H T T R F D W O N H C
D E T L R J N B D R U P M J T G B F S I M G T O K M H T S V G H Y
O J U T R E F D M L O U Y T R E M G D W O U N N K J G R T H N E
K W K M H Y T H K U R G F E O N H R L L O I G T E F R E H Y T R S

Things to Do

- ☐ *If you have told a lie recently, go to the person you lied to and tell them the truth.*
- ☐ *Always tell the whole truth (partial truths are still lies).*
- ☐ *Read Proverbs 11. Choose one of the proverbs about honesty and write about a time in your life when it was proved true.*
- ☐ *Make a poster displaying the benefits of honesty to help you remember to be honest.*

do it

Things to Remember

Yes, what joy for those whose record the LORD has cleared of guilt, whose lives are lived in complete honesty! — *Psalm 32:2*

You desire honesty from the womb, teaching me wisdom even there. — *Psalm 51:6*

Honesty guides good people; dishonesty destroys treacherous people. — *Proverbs 11:3*

The godly are directed by honesty; the wicked fall beneath their load of sin. — *Proverbs 11:5*

And the seeds that fell on the good soil represent honest, good-hearted people who hear God's word, cling to it, and patiently produce a huge harvest. — *Luke 8:15*

wisdom

No man has a good enough memory to make a successful liar.
— *Abraham Lincoln*

A half-truth is a whole lie.
— *Yiddish Proverb*

There's one way to find out if a man is honest—ask him. If he says, "Yes," you know he is a crook.
— *Groucho Marx*

Laughing Your Face Off

Sarah declared, "God has brought me laughter. All who hear about this will laugh with me."
Genesis 21:6

Nick had a tough life. He wasn't doing well in school. He mowed lawns and cleaned yards to help his dad buy food. He lived with his dad and two younger sisters. They didn't have much money, and even though Nick tried to help, his family always had it rough. This made Nick sad. He wanted things to be better, but he didn't know what to do. He even cried when no one was looking. He wouldn't do that in front of his dad or sisters because he wanted to be strong for them.

One day he saw his youngest sister, Kathy, crying, and he tried to make her feel better by telling her that he was going to work extra hard so she could get a new toy. But Kathy told Nick she was sad about something else. Nick asked her, "What are you sad about then?" Kathy replied, "I'm sad because you're sad. You don't laugh anymore." Nick realized she was right. He sat there awhile. Then he started tickling Kathy, and Kathy laughed.

Sometimes life can be hard, and it might be easy to get sad and upset, but you should never stop laughing. It's hard to feel sad when you're laughing, and laughing can help other people feel better too. Even in tough times, laughter can be the medicine that breaks the sad moods. God made laughter, and even though you might not think of it very often, God laughs too. Jesus has a sense of humor just like you do. Where do you think you got it from?

When life gets tough, that may be the best time to start laughing. If things are a bit hard and you can't laugh, then at least have fun. Throw the football around or play the new NBA video game with your brother. Go outside and run around with friends. Everyone needs a break from time to time, and that's true for you, too. There's nothing wrong with laughing your face off every so often.

Dear God, thank you for creating laughter. Please help me to keep my spirits up when life gets tough.

Laughter is the best medicine.

Word Search

LAUGHING   FOOTBALL   MOODS   MEDICINE   HUMOR   LAWNS
YARDS   FOOD   MONEY   BROTHER   SISTER   FUN

```
D B D K U T I E A E P T U E J L M
S U T G E F O O T B A L L C U T Y
G V S I S T E R U E O S L K R A H
I O P T L T G F O O D V B N R N N
Y T R F G A O L S L J H D D P R D
P U M E W S U W D N X F S D N D S
Y G O W Y N R G N G W E D L F O R
E J O T P H F D H M T A U O H Y E
N J D P L U T G H I X V L R U W Y
O O S I N L E K J T N S B B M R P
M G F Q B O F J R Y G G I F O Y N
V M E N I C I D E M L E P I R R P
W S Q A D F K N J H G Y T U R W D
K F J G U B R O T H E R G G T T E
```

Secret Code

A B C D E F G H I J K L M N O P Q R S T U V W X Y Z
≈ ´ ! @ # $ % ^ & * ( ) " Ï = + Ω ç √ ∫ Δ © ∂ β å π

—— —— —— —— —— —— —— ——   —— —— —— —— ——
) ≈ Δ % ^ ∫ # ç   ! ≈ Ï ´ #

—— —— —— —— ——   —— —— —— —— —— —— —— ——
≈ % = = @   " # @ & ! & Ï #

Things to Do

- ☐ *Write down a few jokes you think might make God laugh.*
- ☐ *Think of movies and jokes that always make you laugh, and ask your parents if you can share these with a friend.*
- ☐ *When you are feeling down, do something that makes you feel better, like playing a sport, drawing, or writing.*
- ☐ *With some friends write and put on a comedy show for some younger neighborhood kids.*

do it

Things to Remember

He will once again fill your mouth with laughter and your lips with shouts of joy.
— Job 8:21

We were filled with laughter, and we sang for joy. And the other nations said, "What amazing things the Lᴏʀᴅ has done for them."
— Psalm 126:2

wisdom

God blesses you who are hungry now, for you will be satisfied. God blesses you who weep now, for in due time you will laugh. *— Luke 6:21*

May God be merciful and bless us. May his face smile with favor on us. *— Psalm 67:1*

Truth springs up from the earth, and righteousness smiles down from heaven. *— Psalm 85:11*

I am thankful for laughter, except when milk comes out of my nose.
— Woody Allen

Laughter is an instant vacation.
— Milton Berle

Laughter is the sun that drives winter from the human face. *— Victor Hugo*

The Tale of a Short Boy

Devin was different from most kids. He was born deaf, so he often talked louder and in a way that most kids his age had never heard before. He was different, but he didn't let it bother him. Every so often a few boys would make fun of Devin when he wasn't looking. Devin didn't know this, but the other kids did. As the school year went on, the boys started mocking Devin even more, but they made one big mistake—they did it in front of Shane Banks. Shane Banks was a short little boy who looked like he might belong in a younger grade, but he was spunky.

He didn't like it when people teased other kids, and he really didn't like these boys laughing at Devin. As soon as he heard them making fun of Devin, Shane spoke up. In fact, he spoke up loudly. He stood on the cafeteria table and yelled at the boys, telling them how mean they were. He then asked all the other students if they thought the boys teasing Devin were being mean too. The other kids in the room began to get more upset at the mean boys. They all thought the mean boys were doing something wrong, but none of them had the boldness to speak up. When Shane did, the rest of them followed. The mean boys were embarrassed and never messed with Devin again.

God wants his people to be bold and to stand up for him and for things that are right. More people think like you do than you might realize, but most won't speak out unless they know they're not alone. Being bold is not being mean, but being willing to stand up for what's right. This means that you care more about what God thinks than what other people might think of you. It is not always easy, but God likes it. Look around—there may be people at your school that *you* need to stick up for!

pray

Dear God, please give me the boldness necessary to stick up for others and for what's right.

A lot of people know what's right—they are just afraid to say it.

Crossword

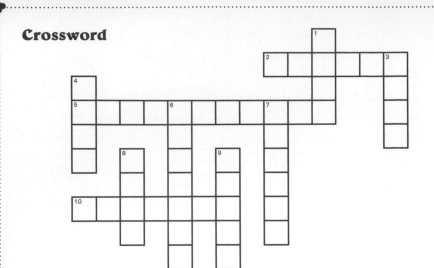

ACROSS

2 If you stand up for someone, it shows you care more about pleasing God than pleasing _____

5 After Shane spoke up, the mean boys were _____

10 Shane did not like the boys _____ Devin

DOWN

1 God wants his people to be _____

3 Being bold is not always _____, but God likes it

4 In the story Devin was born _____

6 More people think like you do than you might _____

7 Shane was short, but he was _____

8 Being bold is not being _____, but being willing to stand up for what's right

9 We should stand up for things that are _____

"I know what he's doing is wrong, but it's hard to stand up for what's right."

Things to Do

☐ *Try this week to tell your friends about God.*

☐ *Ask your parents what kinds of things they think are the most important to speak up about.*

☐ *The next time you hear someone teasing someone else, tell them to stop it.*

☐ *Read Acts 4, which details the apostles' bold stand for Jesus and their prayer for courage.*

do it

Things to Remember

The members of the council were amazed when they saw the boldness of Peter and John, for they could see that they were ordinary men with no special training in the Scriptures. They also recognized them as men who had been with Jesus. – *Acts 4:13*

Because of Christ and our faith in him, we can now come boldly and confidently into God's presence. – *Ephesians 3:12*

I fully expect and hope that I will never be ashamed, but that I will continue to be bold for Christ, as I have been in the past. And I trust that my life will bring honor to Christ, whether I live or die. – *Philippians 1:20*

I am not ashamed of this Good News about Christ. It is the power of God at work, saving everyone who believes—the Jew first and also the Gentile. – *Romans 1:16*

I am in chains now, still preaching this message as God's ambassador. So pray that I will keep on speaking boldly for him, as I should. – *Ephesians 6:20*

wisdom

Freedom lies in being bold.
– *Robert Frost*

Fortune favors the bold. – *Virgil*

Act honestly, and answer boldly.
– *Danish Proverb*

Whispers and Screams

read it

*The earnest prayer
of a righteous
person has great
power and produces
wonderful results.*
James 5:16

Snake Eyes is a ninja master in *G.I. Joe*. He is one of the greatest fighters on the entire team. He also has one of the coolest uniforms. But despite all of his great talents, he doesn't talk. In the comics it's because his vocal cords were injured, while in the movie it's because of the promise he made after his master was killed. Either way, Snake Eyes doesn't speak to those close to him.

What if your mouth were zipped shut and you couldn't talk at all? How would you feel if all your friends and family members couldn't talk to you either? Life might get just a little lonely if you couldn't talk to the people you care about. Communication is important because it's how you tell your parents that you love them or if something is wrong. God made you able to interact with the people you care about.

God likes to hear from you, too. How can you talk to God? You talk to God by praying. You can tell him anything you want. You can talk to him whenever you want to. If you're scared at night, you can whisper to him from under your covers. If you're excited because you just won your baseball game, you can scream a big thank-you to him as loud as you want. God loves to hear from you.

Prayer is important for several reasons. One, it helps you communicate with God, telling him your needs and thoughts. Jesus said that if earthly fathers listen to their children and care for their needs, God the Father will do so even more! Also, when you pray it can actually make a difference. The Bible says that "the earnest prayer of a righteous person has great power." You can pray to tell God how awesome he is. You like to hear when you do a good job, right? So if you get a new video game, or go to Disneyland, or just get to buy a pizza, take time to pray and thank God for everything you have.

Dear God, thank you for letting me talk to you. Please speak to me and help me remember to talk to you.

Secret Codes

Cross out every B, C, F, J, M, N, Q, U, V, X, and Z to solve the secret code.

M N U V P B F X Z R J N C B U X A B Z Q U N J F M N Y N M J C X
Z Q U E B J M N F Q R J M Q U V X B C F I J V X Z C B S N Q H B C
M Q U V Z X O B F J N M Q W B C J B C U V X W Z V U M N J F C
B E B J M N U V T A V U Z Q U L J M N C F B K Q U V X Z C F J M N
Q U V X T B C F J N Q U X C F J O U V X N M J F C F G M N Q U V X
Z J F C B C F J M N Q U X V X Z B C F O J M N Q U V X Z Q N M D

_____ _____ ____ _____ ____ _____ ____ _____ ____ _____

Use the key to solve the secret code.

_____ _____ _____ _____ _____ _____ _____ _____
17 18 22 27 39 14 29 37 34 24 39 25 31 11 24 27

_____ _____ _____ _____ _____
23 24 26 22 24 19 25 15 15 22 34 22 27 11 22

A=24	G=33	M=23	S=28	Y=39
B=36	H=18	N=27	T=31	Z=21
C=11	I=25	O=14	U=29	
D=19	J=30	P=37	V=35	
E=22	K=26	Q=13	W=17	
F=15	L=16	R=34	X=38	

"Dear God, help me say the right thing to Joey."

236

Things to Do

- [ ] *Right now, thank God for all the good things in your life.*
- [ ] *Pray to God throughout the day. For example, ask for help before a test. And then thank him when it's over with.*
- [ ] *Pray for your parents and friends. Do not just pray for yourself.*
- [ ] *Read Jesus' teaching on prayer in Matthew 6 and try it out for yourself.*

do it

Things to Remember

wisdom

Rejoice in our confident hope. Be patient in trouble, and keep on praying. — *Romans 12:12*

And you are helping us by praying for us. Then many people will give thanks because God has graciously answered so many prayers for our safety. — *2 Corinthians 1:11*

Bless those who persecute you. Don't curse them; pray that God will bless them.
— *Romans 12:14*

Keep on asking, and you will receive what you ask for. Keep on seeking, and you will find. Keep on knocking, and the door will be opened to you. For everyone who asks, receives. Everyone who seeks, finds. And to everyone who knocks, the door will be opened.
— *Matthew 7:7-8*

Dear brothers and sisters, I urge you in the name of our Lord Jesus Christ to join in my struggle by praying to God for me. Do this because of your love for me, given to you by the Holy Spirit. — *Romans 15:30*

To be a Christian without prayer is no more possible than to be alive without breathing.
— *Martin Luther King Jr.*

Pray, and let God worry.
— *Martin Luther*

Pray as though everything depended on God. Work as though everything depended on you.
— *Saint Augustine*

Watching Paint Dry

read it

We prove ourselves by our purity, our understanding, our patience, our kindness, by the Holy Spirit within us, and by our sincere love.

2 Corinthians 6:6

Jackson was the worst player on his baseball team. When he got up to bat, he nearly always struck out because he swung at everything. Coach tried to tell him to be patient, but Jackson didn't listen—he just wanted to hit the ball.

Jackson hadn't hit the ball all year. In fact, he hadn't hit the ball in nearly three years. The ball had hit *him* a couple of times, but that hardly counted. Jackson dreamed of being a hero, but with every strikeout that dream seemed more unlikely. The play-offs began, but Jackson knew he wouldn't get a chance to play. But then several of Jackson's teammates got food poisoning at a taco stand the night before the championship game, and there was no one else to start. So Coach put Jackson in the game.

By the ninth inning the game was tied and there were two outs. Jackson was up to bat. Coach told Jackson to be patient and not to swing until the pitcher threw at least one strike. Jackson didn't want to, but he listened to Coach. The pitcher walked Jackson and put him on first base. The next batter hit a single, and Jackson ran all the way to third base. Jackson was so excited he almost didn't see the pitcher throw the ball over the catcher's head. Jackson ran to home plate, but the catcher recovered the ball and was waiting for him. They collided and the ball came loose. Jackson was safe—he was the hero of the game! If Jackson hadn't been patient at the plate, he wouldn't have scored the winning run.

God needs you to be patient because he has good plans for you. But if you rush all the time, you could miss what he has in store for you. Joseph eventually became a powerful leader in Egypt, but only after being in prison for years. Had Joseph not been patient and trusted God, he never would've risen to power like he did. Being patient can seem as boring as watching paint dry, but God promises that good things come to those who wait.

Dear God, please help me to be patient for the good things you have in store for me.

"God, give me patience—right now!"

Secret Code

```
  24    2   12      14   12    6   12   14   14   14   18
  +9  +12   +7     +23  +22   +8  +11  +11  +14   +8  +10
 ____  ____ ____   ____ ____ ____ ____ ____ ____ ____ ____


  18    7   10   18       16   11    7    9
 +13  +11  +14  +13      +17   +3   +7  +10
 ____  ____ ____ ____    ____ ____ ____ ____


  11   16   11   20   13   12        5   12   19   18       16    9
 +20   +2  +14   +7  +20  +16       +6   +2   +4   +4      +15   +5
 ____  ____ ____ ____ ____ ____    ____ ____ ____ ____     ____ ____


  20   12    6   12   14       14   14    9       11    6   10   20
 +11   +6   +8  +16   +8       +3   +4   +5       +6  +18  +15  +11
 ____  ____ ____ ____ ____    ____ ____ ____     ____ ____ ____ ____
```

A=24	G=33	M=23	S=28	Y=39
B=36	H=18	N=27	T=31	Z=21
C=11	I=25	O=14	U=29	
D=19	J=30	P=37	V=35	
E=22	K=26	Q=13	W=17	
F=15	L=16	R=34	X=38	

"Waiting isn't always bad, I guess."

Things to Do

- [ ] *Practice being patient by putting together a big puzzle with one of your siblings.*
- [ ] *Practice being patient by teaching a younger brother or sister a new game. Do not get upset or angry; just take your time.*
- [ ] *Look up the word "patient" in the dictionary and read the different meanings of the word. Write the definitions down, along with how you do and don't fit the description.*
- [ ] *Ask God for patience—and be prepared when he answers!*

do it

Things to Remember

wisdom

Patience can persuade a prince, and soft speech can break bones. — *Proverbs 25:15*

Finishing is better than starting. Patience is better than pride. — *Ecclesiastes 7:8*

May God, who gives this patience and encouragement, help you live in complete harmony with each other, as is fitting for followers of Christ Jesus. — *Romans 15:5*

We also pray that you will be strengthened with all his glorious power so you will have all the endurance and patience you need. — *Colossians 1:11*

But the Holy Spirit produces this kind of fruit in our lives: love, joy, peace, patience, kindness, goodness, faithfulness, gentleness, and self-control.
— *Galatians 5:22-23*

All human wisdom is summed up in two words—wait and hope.
— *Alexandre Dumas*

Patience is the companion of wisdom.
— *Saint Augustine*

Patience serves as a protection against wrongs as clothes do against cold.
— *Leonardo da Vinci*

Puzzle Answers

MR. BIG MOUTH–Page 4

Word Search:

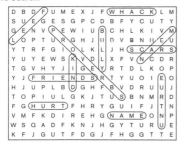

Secret Code: NO ONE LIKES A BULLY.

SWIMMING WITH DUMBBELLS–Page 8

Crossword Puzzle:

DAVID AND THE CHEESE–Page 12

Secret Code: GOD HONORS YOUR OBEDIENCE.

Unscramble These Words: OBEY • GOLIATH • CHEESE • BOSS • DAVID • SHEEP • ARMY

THE DIFFERENCE BETWEEN *OOPS*, *OUCH*, AND *WOW*–Page 16

Unscramble These Words: MISLED • MOCK • JUSTICE • ALWAYS • PLANT

Secret Code: WE WILL REAP A HARVEST OF BLESSING IF WE DO NOT GIVE UP.

"HELP ME, OBI-WAN KENOBI!"–Page 20

Crossword Puzzle:

SINGING PRAISE–Page 24

Word Search:

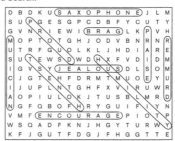

Secret Code: GOD OPPOSES THE PROUD BUT FAVORS THE HUMBLE.

HOW NOT TO BE A SUPER WIMP–Page 28

Secret Code: IT TAKES STRENGTH TO SHOW LOVE.

FASTER THAN A SPEEDING HUG–Page 32

Secret Code: KINDNESS HAS THE POWER TO MELT MEAN HEARTS.

UP, UP, AND AWAY!–Page 36

Word Search:

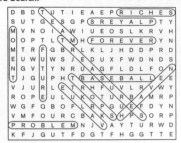

THE STEPLADDER–Page 40

Word Search:

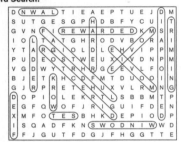

Secret Code: GOD REWARDS THOSE WHO ARE FAITHFUL.

THE TRUTH ABOUT A SPONGE–Page 44

Crossword Puzzle:

SUPER AVERAGE MAN–Page 48

Unscramble These Words: HOMELESS • HELPING • RICH • POOR • KINGDOM • NOTHING • AVERAGE • FOOD • BEGGING • MONEY • SHOCKED

Secret Code: WHEN YOU HELP OTHERS, YOU ARE HELPING GOD.

TURTLENATOR–Page 52

Secret Code: ALWAYS GIVE YOUR BEST.

YOUR SUPERPOWER–Page 56

Crossword Puzzle:

GOING TO GRANDMA'S HOUSE–Page 60

Secret Code: GOD WANTS US TO SHOW COMPASSION

REALITY TV–Page 64

Secret Code: GOD SEES EVERYTHING YOU DO.

Secret Code: GOD EVEN KNOWS WHAT YOU THINK.

A BIKE STORY–Page 68

Word Search:

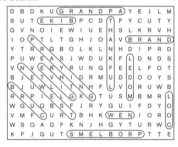

Secret Code: BE THANKFUL FOR WHAT YOU HAVE.

MEGATROUBLE–Page 72

Unscramble These Words: CONTENT • CONSUMED • MEGATRON • DRUG • STARVING • THIRSTY • CONTROL • HUNGER • POWER • DESIRE • TROUBLE • SATISFIED

Secret Code: LET GOD TAKE CARE OF WHAT YOU DON'T HAVE.

BEING A TEAM PLAYER–Page 76

Crossword Puzzle:

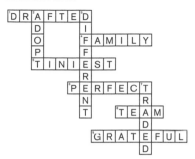

SKUNK FACE–Page 80

Secret Code: HANGING WITH THE WRONG PEOPLE CAN GET YOU IN TROUBLE.

Secret Code: BAD COMPANY CORRUPTS GOOD CHARACTER.

LIP DRIPS–Page 84

Word Search:

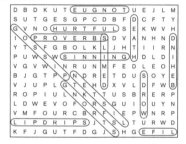

TOUCHDOWN FEVER–Page 88

Unscramble These Words: CONTROL • LOSE • WIN • THANK • CHRISTIAN • ODDS • FOOTBALL • PRESEASON • TRYING • CARDINALS • AWARDS • HURT • YOUNGER

Secret Code: MAKE SURE YOU NEVER GIVE UP.

BEAM ME UP–Page 92

Crossword Puzzle:

PILLOW FIGHTER–Page 96

Word Search:

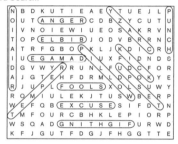

A STILL LOUD VOICE–Page 100

Secret Code: LEARN TO LISTEN TO YOUR CONSCIENCE.

Unscramble These Words: CONSCIENCE • DANGER • PATH • CAVE • SILENT • TROUBLE • MISTAKE • WARNING

THE YELLOW BRICK ROAD–Page 104

Secret Code: WHEN YOU GET DISAPPOINTED ASK GOD FOR HELP.

Secret Code: IN REALITY LIFE CAN BE TOUGH.

SUPER BOOK–Page 108

Secret Code: GOD'S WORD IS A LAMP TO GUIDE MY FEET.

Secret Code: MOST CHEATERS GET CAUGHT.

CHALKBOARD VOICES–Page 112

Crossword Puzzle:

TO BOLDLY GO . . .–Page 116

Word Search:

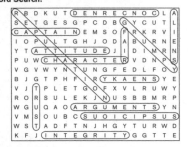

Secret Code: GOD CARES ABOUT YOUR CHARACTER.

SAFETY NET TRAPEZE–Page 120

Secret Code: GET IN THE HABIT OF FOLLOWING RULES.

MAZED AND CONFUSED–Page 124

Word Search:

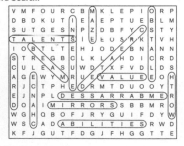

Secret Code: YOU ARE ALWAYS VALUABLE TO GOD.

A SNAIL MYSTERY–Page 128

Secret Code: JESUS CAME TO EARTH AS A BABY.

A KING AND HIS HORSES–Page 132

Crossword Puzzle:

SAMSON AND HIS HAIR–Page 136

Secret Code: REMEMBER: GOD HAS YOUR BACK.

Secret Code: LOOK TO GOD IN TOUGH TIMES.

A SQUID'S GUIDE TO WHAT NOT TO DO–
Page 140

Word Search:

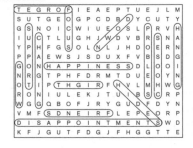

BUILDING TREE HOUSES–Page 144

Unscramble These Words: DISCIPLINE • PARENTS • TEACHERS • PASTORS • LOVE • MATURE • HEAVEN • TALENTS • PINCHED

Secret Code: HONEST DISCIPLINE IS A FORM OF LOVE.

REACH FOR THE STARS–Page 148

Secret Code: HEAVEN IS A REALLY AWESOME PLACE.

Secret Code: YOU WILL MEET JESUS FACE TO FACE IN HEAVEN.

THE CLOWN AND THE COWBOY—Page 152

Word Search:

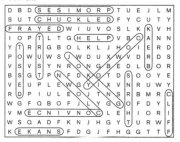

Secret Code: GOD WANTS YOU TO TRUST HIM AND OTHERS TO TRUST YOU.

WAR OF THE WORLDS—Page 156

Crossword Puzzle:

WILD WILD WEST—Page 160

Secret Code: YOU CAN WORSHIP GOD ANYWHERE.

VIDEO GAME CHAMPIONS—Page 164

Secret Code: LEARN FROM THE PEOPLE AROUND YOU.

Secret Code: GOD KNEW YOU WOULD NEED HELP.

SWIMMING PALS—Page 168

Word Search:

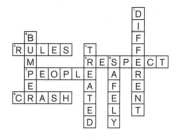

Secret Code: DO YOUR BEST TO MAKE THINGS RIGHT.

STOP SIGNS—Page 172

Crossword Puzzle:

THE FIRE SWAMP—Page 176

Secret Code: THE BIBLE SAYS THAT YOU REAP WHAT YOU SOW.

Secret Code: CARE FOR THE NEEDS OF OTHERS.

CAR WASH SUNDAYS—Page 180

Unscramble These Words: SIN • CHURCH • PRIORITY • WASHED • CLEANED • TIME • HANGING • MUSTANGS • DIRTY • IMPACT • HELPING

Secret Code: GOING TO CHURCH SHOWS THAT GOD IS A PRIORITY.

THE COWARDLY LION—Page 184

Secret Code: GOD CAN HELP YOU HAVE MORE COURAGE.

THE CAKE MONSTER—Page 188

Secret Code: EATING RIGHT IS JUST PART OF STAYING HEALTHY.

THE GAME OF SORRY–Page 192

Crossword Puzzle:

WATERFALLS AND DIAPERS–Page 196

Secret Code: WHEN GOD MAKES SOMETHING, HE DOES IT RIGHT.

Secret Code: GOD CREATED SO MANY AMAZING THINGS FOR YOU TO ENJOY.

NO LAUGHING MATTER–Page 200

Unscramble These Words: HUMOR • PROUD • JOKES • BOUNDARIES • BASKETBALL • MEAN • TOUGHER • INSECURE • OLDER

Secret Code: A REAL MAN DOES NOT NEED TO TELL BAD JOKES.

ROLLER COASTERS, HOCKEY, AND LEARNING HOW TO LOSE–Page 204

Word Search:

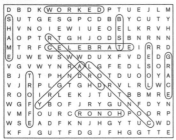

Secret Code: EVERYONE RESPECTS A GOOD LOSER.

BALLOON HEADS–Page 208

Secret Code: DON'T BE A BALLOON HEAD.

Secret Code: IT IS IMPORTANT TO WIN WITH CLASS.

THE BUYING FLU–Page 212

Crossword Puzzle:

THE NORTH STAR OF LIFE–Page 216

Secret Code: JESUS CAN ALWAYS SHOW YOU THE RIGHT PATH.

SCROOGE GETS ROBBED–Page 220

Word Search:

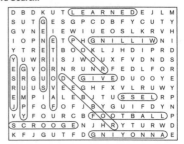

TRUTH OR DARE–Page 224

Secret Code: LYING ONLY GETS YOU IN MORE TROUBLE.

Secret Code: IT IS HARD FOR PEOPLE TO TRUST SOMEONE WHO LIES.

LAUGHING YOUR FACE OFF–Page 228

Word Search:

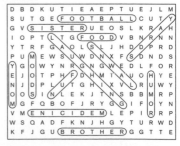

Secret Code: LAUGHTER CAN BE A GOOD MEDICINE.

THE TALE OF A SHORT BOY–Page 232

Crossword Puzzle:

WHISPERS AND SCREAMS–Page 236

Secret Code: PRAYER IS HOW WE TALK TO GOD.

Secret Code: WHEN YOU PRAY IT CAN MAKE A DIFFERENCE.

WATCHING PAINT DRY–Page 240

Secret Code: GOD PROMISES THAT GOOD THINGS COME TO THOSE WHO WAIT.